Walk with Me
through the
INTERNET

Dear Mr. Hutzel,

You are right! See page 45.

Come walk with me...

Enjoy! 😊

Andrew, Class of 1996

P.S. Thanks for the great advice Mr. Hutzel & all the fun & exciting history classes too. Do you remember my paper "The Hippie Trip"?

Walk with Me
—— through the ——
INTERNET

An easy and enlightening guide to using and
understanding the Internet for newcomers

Andrew Gold

Sunshine Daydream Press San Francisco 1998

www.walkwithme.com

Copyright © 1998 Andrew Gold.

All rights reserved.

Printed in the United States of America. No part of this book
may be used or reproduced in any manner whatsoever
without written permission except in the case of
brief quotations embodied in critical
articles and reviews.

Published by:
Sunshine Daydream Press
227 Cole Street
San Francisco, CA 94117
http://www.sunshinedaydream.com

ISBN 0–9662865–0–2

This book is printed on recycled paper. Sunshine Daydream is committed
to using paper with the highest recycled content
available consistent with high quality.

This guide is dedicated to
my Mom and Dad,
Nancy and David Gold.

They have spent so many years
showing me the way.
With this guide, I thought
I could return a little of the favor.

CONTENTS

ACKNOWLEDGEMENTS ix

PREFACE xi

1 Mom and Dad, come walk with me. 1

2 BANG! The Internet revolution begins. 5

3 Getting online: a few simple steps 9

4 The Big Three: E-mail, the Web, and Usenet 23

5 The Internet? The Web? What's the difference? 29

6 E-mail—Simple, quick, easy, cheap 39

7 Browsing the Web 49

8 Newsgroups—The Hidden Gem of the Internet 59

9 Finding everything you're looking for: The Search Engines 67

10 The Heart and Soul of the Web 71

11 On the Horizon 83

A Friendly Glossary 87

Acknowledgements

A special thank you to all the friends and family who graciously assisted me by providing helpful feedback and suggestions about my initial manuscript.

I owe my gratitude to this adventurous crew (listed in alphabetical order): Milton Aronson, Carol Fields, Jenny Friesenhahn, Carolyn Gold, David Gold, Nancy Gold, and Divanilda Patriota. After I wrote the first version of the manuscript I called upon this select group of Internet newcomers to read through it and note any unclear areas. I was pleasantly surprised by both the precision of their comments and insights as well as the promptness of their replies.

Thanks, Mom, for helping me pick out the right title for this guide. It certainly is an improvement over the original one.

And of course I owe my thanks to Terry and Sandy Lillie and the whole crew at OMIX, Inc. I have learned so much from each and every one of you. A big thank you to Harold Sasaki who helped guide me through the Internet in the beginning and to Jackie Piercy for her improvements to this guide.

Thank you also to my past colleagues in the technical support department of Dantz Development Inc., especially Joanne Kalogeras, Lars Holmes, and Zef Correal.

Thanks to Ken Debono and the Falcon Books team for their production advice and expert hands-on knowledge. You have tranformed my good ideas into an even better book.

And to all who continue to make Sunshine Daydream so bright, I give a huge high five.

Preface

I wrote this book for my parents. And for you too. My parents are both working professionals who have passed many happy years of their lives without computers or the Internet. Perhaps you can relate to their situation. Their feelings about this new world range from intrigue to hesitation, confusion, and intimidation.

I want to show you the Internet you can understand. I wrote this guide in your language. It is directed at newcomers who want to learn about this amazing new world of the Internet. In a fun way I will show you what it is and how you can use it. We'll start from the beginning.

I think the Internet is pretty cool. As a professional, I architect information for a premier Internet technologies development company, OMIX, Inc., where I am surrounded by people who have a deep understanding of the Internet's inner workings. In addition, I produce the web site Sunshine Daydream, the source for outdoor adventures in the San Francisco Bay Area.

On a realistic note, it took me months, even years, to accumulate the knowledge that I am sharing with you. Please have patience with yourself as you learn more and more. I recommend reading through this whole guide (it's less than 90 pages!) to get a good feel for what's ahead. Then you can turn back to a particular section as it applies to your specific journey. My mantra: *Always appreciate how much you have learned rather than fret about what you still do not know (but will soon enough!).*

Let's turn this fearful task into a comfortable and pleasant adventure. Come along...

1

Mom and Dad, come walk with me.

The sun shall not be up so soon as I,
To try the fair adventure of tomorrow.
WILLIAM SHAKESPEARE
1564—1616

Hi Mom and Dad, and other newcomers to the Internet arena, I hope you like fun adventures. We're going on a quick one, to a new place which all of you have heard about, and may have seen a little too. I'll be your tour guide, and I promise to point you in the right direction, as all good guides do. After we're done, you'll have the insight and knowledge to be able to continue the journey on your own, finding your own trails. This adventure will challenge you a bit (as all good adventures should!), but there are ample rewards for your efforts.

What is the **Internet**? The Internet is a worldwide system of computers connected together, the information on those computers, and the people all over the world accessing and sharing that information. Relax, you don't have to "learn computers" to use the Internet, just as you don't have to get under the hood of your car to drive it. You only have to press buttons and steer—and that's the fun part!

Before the Internet, the average person was simply a consumer of information. The information which comes to us by way of TV, radio, and newspaper had no real feedback channel besides the occasional letter to the editor, phone call to the radio station, and other minor loops. The message was sent, and we merely received it. Now, with this new communication tool, a beautiful world is coming alive: PARTICIPATION. The Internet beseeches us to connect with others, provide our opinions, control the information which comes to us, and interact with it at all stages.

So you may be thinking to yourself, "Great. As if learning how to use a computer isn't hard enough, now I also have to deal with this computerized Internet blitz." I think you'll be glad to find out that the Internet is not just one more tedious exercise with computers with little reward at the end. The good news is that lots of companies have worked (and are still working) really hard to make your computer as easy as possible to use. And if you've delayed getting online, it's even easier today to connect than it was a year ago.

The Hype

So, what do I say about all the hype? First, let's take a look at the definition of hype. The American Heritage® Dictionary provides two straightforward definitions:

1. *intensive publicity and the ensuing commotion.*
2. *exaggerated or extravagant claims made especially in advertising or promotional material.*

The second definition comes a lot closer to the reason for all the Internet hype—everyone's trying to sell you something, from faster computers to quicker modems to easier software to new products, to newspapers and magazines. Internet hype has been ringing in our ears for about two years now. I'll show you a good path through it so that your blood pressure will remain low. The fact of the matter is, the main computer programs which you use for the Internet are really easy to learn and once you get going, you'll do fine. I promise.

The Internet is a nice tool you can use to find resources and make connections to all kinds of people in all kinds of places. Want to know more about an area of interest to you? You'll find it and a lot more on the Internet.

Let's get perspective.

How do you deal best with the "hype?" The answer is by getting perspective. Let's go to a high peak so we can see the Internet from above. When my friends and family come to San Francisco to visit me, I always take them to Twin Peaks, the highest of the hills in San Francisco. From this majestic place, you can see all of the city, the Golden Gate Bridge, the Headlands beyond, the Bay Bridge, Alcatraz, the TransAmerica building, Candlestick Park, Oakland, the Pacific Ocean, the Bay, Golden Gate Park, and several other special places, hills and valleys in the area. There is something wonderful which you gain at Twin Peaks—PERSPECTIVE. I'm going to bring you to the top, so you can see the Internet from above. Then, you'll be able to sightsee on your own.

If you just go into a book store and read all the titles of the Internet books, you'll see a different view from each author. Why listen to me? I believe in simplicity and reducing seemingly complicated systems into bite size chunks. And I hate wasting time. Yours or mine.

In a few pages I will:

- *show you how to get connected to the Internet, quickly and easily*
- *show you how to use the Internet to meet your needs*
- *give you an insider's view so you can see the hype for what the hype really is*
- *help you understand the bigger picture, where we are now, and where we're going*

Most importantly, I'm leaving out the stuff you don't need to know.

A Quick Word about the Lingo

It's really hard to talk about this new world of the Internet without mentioning the common terms. In this manual I have avoided the "techy talk" where possible and have included a handful of the most important words which will help you understand the Internet better. The first time these words appear they'll be bolded like this: **Internet**. Then I'll give you a clear description of the new term. For reference, there's a glossary at the end of this book which you can turn to at any point.

2

BANG! The Internet revolution begins.

A whole is that which has beginning, middle and end.
ARISTOTLE
384–322 BCE

> This is just a quick overview. In chapter 5 I'll give the real details behind the history and growth of the Internet and the Web.

Isn't it funny how quickly the Internet wave crashed down on us? From 1969, when the Internet first started, to 1994, 99% of America and the world couldn't have cared less about it. Today, everywhere we look we can't help but see those **web addresses**, like http://www.ups.com, plastered on vehicles, billboards, TV commercials, radio commercials, business cards and so on.

Back in 1990, there were less than one million Americans **online**. Online means connected to the Internet. In 1995 there were about 5 million Americans online and now, three years later, in 1998 there are over 20 million Americans online. And for the next couple of years, it looks like the growth rate will dramatically increase before slowing down as we enter the next millennium. What happened to cause this explosion?

Answer: the Internet got a face lift. The Internet started to look a lot like magazines. Nice graphics, photographs, and beautiful interfaces replaced boring black-and-white text which was peacefully existing for over twenty years without our attention. Rather than having to know complicated menus, now the average person (like you and me) could just use his or her mouse (I hope you know what a computer mouse is by now!) and click to connect with people and places and information all over the world. You have a world of information at your fingertips! Simple, easy, and fun.

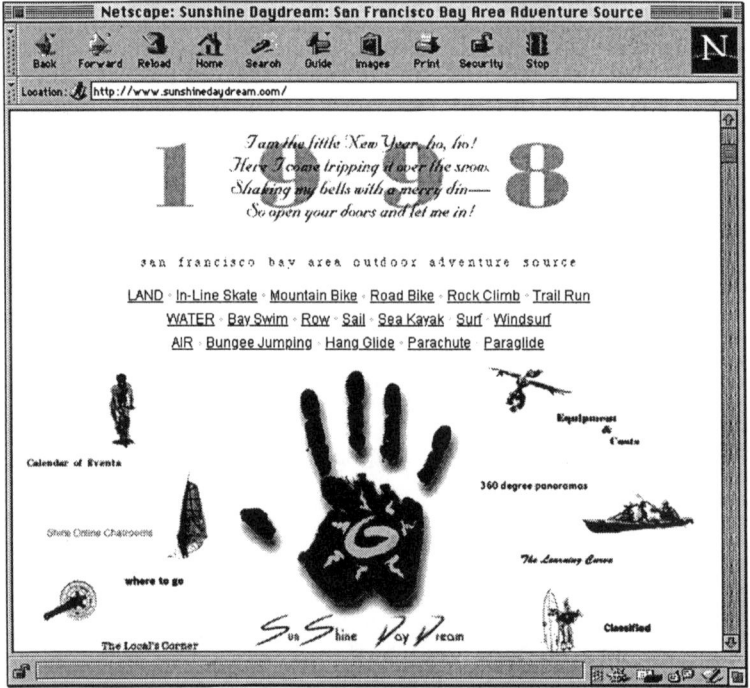

The browser Netscape Navigator™ displaying a web page from the web site Sunshine Daydream.

The word **browser** suddenly entered our vocabulary. The browser is the program used for "browsing around" the Internet to see **web pages**. Web pages are like magazine pages which you see through the browser. A **web site** is a group of these web pages, usually organized by a particular subject or topic. The browser was a revolutionary new tool which could display information throughout this giant worldwide network in the form of both text and photographs or other designs—together. When you open a magazine or even a newspaper this is quite common. The pictures bring the words to life. But for over twenty years you could only read plain text on the Internet without seeing any colorful pictures. What fun is that? The browser was an amazing accomplishment which came about in 1992. The first browsers, made by a couple of programmers, were fun toys given away for free.

Then something amazing happened. In the fall of 1995, Netscape Communication Corp., the company with the most advanced browser, went public and their stock blasted through the stratosphere. Starting at around $20 a share, it jumped up to $80, then $130, then peaked at around $180, all in the first week! Marc Andreesen, the twenty-three year old whiz kid browser programmer, and Jim Clark, the visionary who saw the potential of the browser and the Internet, officially started a revolution. Marc made about $70 million and Jim about $500 million that first week off of the value of their stocks. The race was now on; a resounding BANG! swept throughout the world. The Internet and the Web were real—not just toys anymore—a present-day gold rush for thousands of businesses.

After Netscape went public, countless computer hardware, software, communication, and media companies saw the Internet with big $$ in their eyes. One familiar to everybody is Microsoft. Both big companies, like IBM, Apple, Oracle, Hewlett-Packard, AT&T, and SUN Microsystems, and small new startup companies all wanted to play in the golden sandbox.

With so much talent, money, resources, and competition concentrated in one area, amazing progress was (and still is) made. That is the story of the last couple years. So, now that you are ready to join, please appreciate how hard everyone is working to make your life easier. And the good news is that most of it is FREE! Pretty cool, huh?

But, first things first. Without being connected to the Internet none of this helps you. So, let's go get connected. *Note: you will not have to be connected to learn a lot of what I'm going to show you.*

3

Getting online: a few simple steps

A journey of a thousand miles must begin with one step.
LAO-TZO
C. 604–C. 531 BCE

Getting online simply means using a computer to "talk" to other computers on the Internet. There are several ways you can go about this. You can use someone else's computer or buy your own. The cheapest way is to go to the local library which should already have computers connected to the Internet. You simply ask the librarian where these computers are and where you can sign up to use them. Likewise, college students and high school students have many convenient options to connect through their school.

If you already own a computer but have not used it for the Internet or are thinking about buying a computer, it is easy to get online from both home and the office. Let's take a look at the options so that you can decide what is best for your needs.

Connecting to the Internet from your home or office, you will need:

- *A computer (a keyboard, monitor, and mouse too) and a modem*
- *A telephone line (you can use your existing phone line)*
- *An Internet Service Provider (ISP) or a Commercial Online Service (Compuserve, Prodigy, AOL, MSN)*
- *Some software and info the Internet Service Provider or Commercial Online Service will provide you*
- *Patience*

A computer and a modem

Hardware comprises the physical computer parts which depreciate relentlessly after you buy them. If you can touch it, it is hardware. You know what a computer is as well as a monitor, keyboard, and a mouse. You may not know that a **modem** is an actual little box that plugs into your computer on one end and your telephone line on the other. The modem is what lets your computer "talk" to the computers on the other end of the phone line.

Computers double in speed of operation every two years. Modems are getting faster all the time. What this means is that every year you will have to withstand countless impulses to upgrade your system to the newest and fastest. A tip: enjoy what you have and appreciate it for what it is, rather than for what it is not.

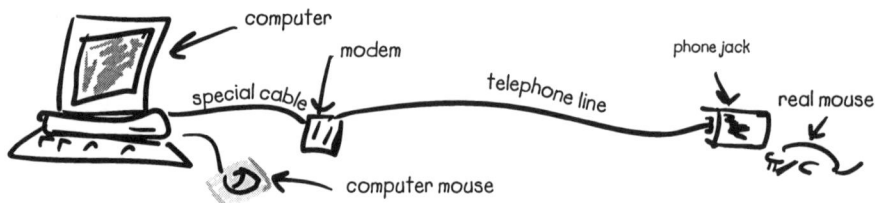

Getting a computer

Choosing the right computer can seem particularly tedious, especially because there are so many different models and vendors. A desktop computer can be large or small, fast or slow, versatile or limited. I look at it this way: everyone is selling the same thing, more or less. Your biggest choice is to decide between a **Mac** (made by Apple Computer which calls its computers Macintoshes or a Mac "clone") and a **PC** or Personal Computer (made by IBM or its "clones"). Regardless of type, for around $1300–$2000 you should be able to get a complete **multimedia system** (computer, monitor, keyboard, mouse and speakers), which comes with a modem too, and is ready to jump right on to the Internet. And, if this is too much, you can always get an older system which can still access the Internet. It may be slower, but it will work.

The Internet is not particularly demanding on a personal computer, so you do not need a big and fast machine to enjoy it. As a matter of fact, some people use computers which are several years old and do just fine. *As long as you can connect a modem to the computer, you can access the Internet.*

I personally prefer the Apple Macintosh, and am still happy with my *Power Mac 7100* which is over two years old and almost three times as slow as the newest models. But nowadays, about 96% of new home computers sold are PCs (operated by Microsoft Windows **operating system**); the remaining 4% are Macs, and the majority of salesmen will be pushing the PC. While we're on the subject, an operating system is a computer program that operates the computer. It's a form of **software** which is code telling the computer what to do and how to behave.

If I were you, I would buy a similar computer to that of a knowledgeable friend who lives close to me. That way, your friend who knows a lot about his or her computer system can help solve your computer problems too. You will have questions along the way, and what could be better than spending some time with a good friend while he or she helps you? The real trick to all this computer stuff is finding other people out there who already know the answers. Why spend a half-day of your precious time dealing with a problem that any experienced user can fix in a few minutes?

Here are few pros and cons of buying either a PC or a Mac:

A PC using the Microsoft Windows operating system

> The majority of desktop computers are PCs. There is more competition, so the prices are a little cheaper and *some* programs are released for the PC first. On the downside, Windows 95 is still not as easy to use as the Mac (although it is pretty user friendly) and you will experience more problems, especially when adding new components. And you must always consider the Microsoft factor. "What's that?" you ask. Let's just say that some of Microsoft's anti-competitive business practices have attracted the attention of consumer advocate Ralph Nader, the Department of Justice, and several other organizations trying to protect our rights as consumers. Less competition equals less choice.

Apple Macintosh

> The Mac is still a much easier computer to use and the graphics are nicer too. One reason they are so easy is that Apple Computers makes both the computer hardware and the operating system. On the downside Macintoshes are the minority. Some cynical folks might say that the threat of extinction looms over the Mac, but this is simply not true. I personally prefer the Macintosh due to its quality, compatibility, and efficiency.

Beware of the hype when buying a computer. They will try to sell you the fastest **processor** (the engine of your computer), the biggest **hard drive** (the place you store your computer programs and files), and the most amount of **RAM** (special memory for running more programs at the same time). You can do just fine with a middle-of-the-road machine. This is where the best deals are. Aren't cars the same? And if you just want to use e-mail, almost *any* old, slow, and inexpensive computer will do. And this is just fine for lots of people, including you.

Middle-of-the-Road Machine

A friend suggested that I list the system requirements for enjoying the whole spectrum of the Internet. I'm briefly going to list some standard features of a middle-of-the-road desktop computer which should cost around $1500:

- 90 to 180 **megahertz** processor (megahertz is millions of operations per second). The fastest processors run at 200–300 megahertz, but you'll pay a lot for these and do not need all that power for the Internet.
- 500 to 1500 **megabytes** (millions of **bytes**—a whole bunch of bits) hard drive. This is the space for storing your computer programs and files.
- 24 **megs** (megabytes) of RAM (remember, RAM is the special memory for running computer programs). Less than this and you will not be able to run more than three standard programs at the same time.
- 15" monitor (13" and 14" are too small and you will strain your eyes)
- 33.6 K modem (I will talk about this shortly)

- Ability to play sound. With Macintosh computers this is a standard feature but a PC may or may not have this ability. Make sure to check.
- Built in CD-ROM. Once again, a standard feature in today's computers.

Suffice it to say that after shopping a little, you will start to recognize the low, middle, and high-end computers by comparing these features and their prices. But don't feel that you need a big powerful system to use the Internet. Not at all. For some of the Internet's greatest features, like e-mail and newsgroups, an old clunker can do just fine.

Getting a modem

The modem connects your computer to the telephone line, and hence the Internet on the other end. You plug your computer into the modem and then plug your modem into your phone line. If you want to impress your friends, tell them the word modem is a contraction for two beefy words: **mo**dulator-**dem**odulator, words that relate to transmission-reception. Just as your phone converts your voice into the signals which go through the phone line, the modem converts the "computer talk" in a similar fashion.

There are simply two factors you need to consider when buying a modem: 1) **internal** or **external** and 2) how fast a speed. Internal/external refers to the actual location of the modem within (internal) or outside (external) your computer. An internal modem is a little less expensive than an external modem and it's easier to carry since it is located inside your computer (laptop computer folks usually get internal modems). The advantage of the external is that you can see little blinking lights when the modem is talking and it is easier to move the modem from one computer to another. Either way, the internal and external modems function the same.

The **K** after the number 28.8 K stands for **kbps** or **kilo (thousands of) bits per second**. Computers talk to each other in **bits** (**binary digits** are 1s and 0s), the more bits the faster. So when they talk about a 28.8 Kbps modem, they mean a 28.8 kilo bits per second or 28,000 bits per second. This is faster than a mere 14,000 bits per second and so on. You'll hear someone say, "My 28.8 K modem is faster than your 14.4 K." Remember, the bigger the number is, the faster the modem talks.

Modems keep getting faster and faster. A year ago the 28.8 K was the fastest and now we have 33.6 K and even 56 K. I still use my 14.4 K. I recommend the middle-of-the-road modem such as the 28.8 K. If the price for the 33.6 K is just a little more than the 28.8 K, I'd go with that. Right now, the 56 K is not as stable and it is much more expensive. Around $100 is a decent price to pay for a modem. If you are buying a brand new computer, it will probably come with a modem and that's one less decision you will have to make.

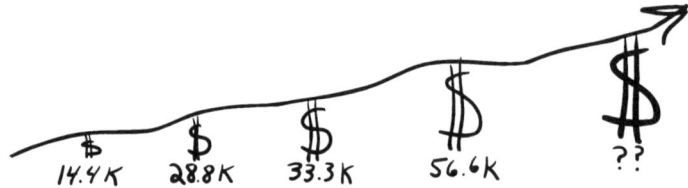

As modem speeds get quicker, the prices go up.

The Guys on the Other End of the Phone Line

The modem connects through a phone line to the Internet. So there has to be someone on the other end of the line. Nowadays, there are lots of companies who would just love to be on the other end of your line for $20 a month, that is. This is actually not a bad price, especially considering they used to charge by the hour. For this $20 a month you get access to the three main Internet services. I'll tell you about these services in the next chapter. Think of this as joining a fitness club. With your membership you get access to their services: the free weights, the running track and the swimming pool. I'm going to build off this analogy so stick with me. For now the free weights, the running track and the swimming pool are analogous to the three main Internet services: e-mail, the Web and Usenet. I describe these in the chapters 6, 7, and 8 respectively.

You have three choices to connect to the Internet nowadays, each with its own pluses and minuses.

1. *A Commercial Online Service. America Online, Compuserve, Prodigy, MSN are the most well known. These all have 800 telephone numbers.*

2. *A national Internet Service Provider (ISP). GTE/BBN Planet, UUNet, AT&T, MCI, Sprint, and Earthlink are examples. These too have 800 telephone numbers.*

3. *A local Internet Service Provider. Each city will have a handful. Consult your local Yellow Pages and look under "Internet".*

Actually, there is one more choice, if you just want **e-mail** or electronic mail. *Note: with these free e-mail services you only get e-mail. Think of this as only getting to use the free weights (going back to our sports club analogy) without use of the running track or the swimming pool.* Within the last couple of years, several free e-mail companies have popped up on the Internet. The two most popular are Juno and Hot Mail. They make their money off of advertising, so they do not charge you for their e-mail service. Both of these services already have millions of loyal users.

To use Juno you only need a computer and a modem. You do not need to pay for your own Internet connection. It may surprise you that you do not need anything else. You can call Juno at 1-800-654-5866 and they'll be happy to tell you all about their service.

If you have access to a computer from the public library or your school, and this computer is connected to the Internet, you can use Hot Mail for your e-mail. You are essentially piggy backing off of someone else's connection to the Internet. You can call Hot Mail at 1-408-222-7000 for information.

The Difference between a Commercial Online Service and an Internet Service Provider (ISP)

A very common question is, "What's the difference between a Commercial Online Service like Compuserve and an Internet Service Provider like AT&T World Net?"

15

Think of the Internet as a bunch of computers all over the world with individual owners who simply place them on the Internet for the rest of the world to access. So, the Internet is like a worldwide street fair of computers and information. No one owns it; they are merely participating in the fair. **Internet Service Providers**, or **ISPs** for short, simply give you access to the street fair (the Internet), but essentially nothing else. Please don't get me wrong, the Internet is a whole lot! Because their only job is Internet connectivity, on the whole, their track record for service, performance and reliability is better than that of the Commercial Online Services which I describe below.

	Commercial Online Service	Internet Service Provider (ISP)
Connection to Internet	Yes	Yes (Usually better)
Special Forums	Yes	NO
Special Rules	Yes (Bad)	No (Good)
Pricing $	around $20/month	around $20/month

A quick comparison of Commercial Online Servers and Internet Service Providers.

Commercial Online Services, like *Prodigy, Compuserve, America Online,* and *MSN*, provide more than just access to this world wide street fair of computers. They have their own special information and computers, in addition to providing access to the Internet. Only their members can access this information. For instance, America Online has a wonderful forum for Judaism (which is headed by a nice man, Marc Klein, the editor of the *Jewish Bulletin Newspaper* in San Francisco). If you are not an America Online member, you can neither access nor participate in this special forum nor any of the other America Online forums for that matter. Prodigy has Prodigy forums, MSN has MSN forums and so on.

In addition, the Commercial Online Services have their own set of rules and their own set of programs too. They make a lot of decisions which you may or may not like, but have no choice but to follow. An Internet Service Provider simply connects you to the Internet without all the extra 1) forums (bad!) and 2) rules (good!).

You may be asking yourself, "If for the same price, around $20 per month, by joining a Commercial Online Service I get everything the Internet Service Providers offer plus a whole lot more, why wouldn't I join a Commercial Online Service?" First of all, the Internet has just about everything imaginable. Sure some of the forums are nice, but when it's all said and done, you'll find something similar (or even better) on the Internet. An Internet Service Provider specializes in simply providing access to the Internet. The overall quality and performance of their Internet connections are higher. On the whole, Internet Service Providers have a better track record of customer satisfaction, and with an Internet Service Provider, you do not have to deal with the Commercial Online Services' rules. Just remember this: there is a trade-off between going with an Internet Service Provider or a Commercial Online Service. Each has its own positives and negatives.

Let me repeat this important information. You can connect to the Internet via:

1. *A Commercial Online Service. America Online, Compuserve, Prodigy, MSN are the most well known.*

2. *A national Internet Service Provider (ISP). GTE/BBN Planet, UUNet, AT&T, MCI, Sprint, and Earthlink are some examples.*

3. *A local Internet Service Provider. Each city will have a handful.*

The Commercial Online Services used to charge by the hour. So you would pay an automatic $10 a month for 10 free hours, then pay something like $3 an hour for each and every additional hour. This is when articles appeared in the paper about folks paying hundreds of dollars a month to American Online because they were addicted to the Internet. This is particularly unfortunate because these poor folks could have simply gotten online with an Internet Service Provider for a flat monthly fee, all-you-can-eat. Nowadays this is the common competitive model. Everyone is offering unlimited Internet access for a flat monthly fee of around $20.

Take the time to find the right Internet Service Provider or Commercial Online Service for you, because there is a good chance that once you get connected, you're not going to want to change. Find a company with an excellent reputation for good customer service.

GOOD CUSTOMER SERVICE is crucial. When you have a problem or can't figure something out, you'll most likely call the technical support line. A good technical support specialist (I used to be one of these) will take the time to walk you through each and every step of setting up your system and troubleshooting your problems. This should be a really big criteria on your list in choosing the right company. My Internet Service Provider in San Francisco, Sirius Connections, has provided me with excellent assistance and this has made a big difference in solving my Internet problems.

Here's a good tip. Call the prospective Internet Service Provider or Commercial Online Service that you are considering and ask them for their technical support number. Give the number a call and see how long it takes to talk with an actual person. When you have a problem, that's how long you'll have to wait to talk to someone who can help you. Would you believe that some services make you wait for hours, even days, before providing technical assistance? More than 10 minutes is too long when you need help.

My Personal Experience

The first time I connected to the Internet was in March of 1995. America Online mailed me a floppy disk. I simply popped the America Online floppy disk into my computer, clicked on the AOL **icon** (a little computer graphic) and a nice program came up asking me a few questions. I provided the answers and chose a **login name** (this becomes your e-mail address) and a **password**. The login name becomes the name of your account. Both your login name and password can be whatever you like, but make sure your password is easy enough for you to remember and hard enough for someone else not to be able to guess.

To my surprise, right then and there, my computer had my modem dial into America Online and I was connected. They automatically provided me with all the programs I needed to use their service and to use the Internet too. It was really easy and fast.

But the $3 an hour (for each hour after the 10 free hours) started taking its financial toll, so a few months later I closed my AOL account and opened an account with an excellent local Internet Service Provider called Sirius Connections which a clerk in a computer bookstore recommended. I called Sirius Connections and they sent me 1) a floppy disc with the programs I needed to connect to the Internet and 2) a little booklet for setting up my computer system. (You might hear the word **configure**, such as, "I configured my computer to get online." Configure means to set up which is a lot less of a mouthful.) The floppy disk with the programs and the booklet arrived a few days later. I just clicked on a few icons and followed their clear directions step by step. It was very straightforward. I called their technical support once with a question which they answered swiftly. With Sirius I chose a login name and a password and was connected to the Internet in about thirty minutes. The process is the same for all the Internet Service Providers.

Beyond Borders

One more little tidbit of info which may be of interest to those of you who travel: your Internet access from the service for which you have paid $20 per month is not confined to your home or office computer. Let me explain the basics.

The Commercial Online Services and Internet Service Providers each have telephone numbers in different locations. You obviously want to connect to the Internet with a local telephone call to avoid long distance charges. Some of these companies, like Prodigy and AT&T World Net, have access telephone numbers all over the country (and the world for that matter). You can get online in all the cities where your service operates with a local telephone call if you have access to a computer there.

These access locations are technically called **points of presence**. I just called up UUNet and found out that they have a point of presence in Milan in addition to San Francisco and most other major US cities. So, if you get online with

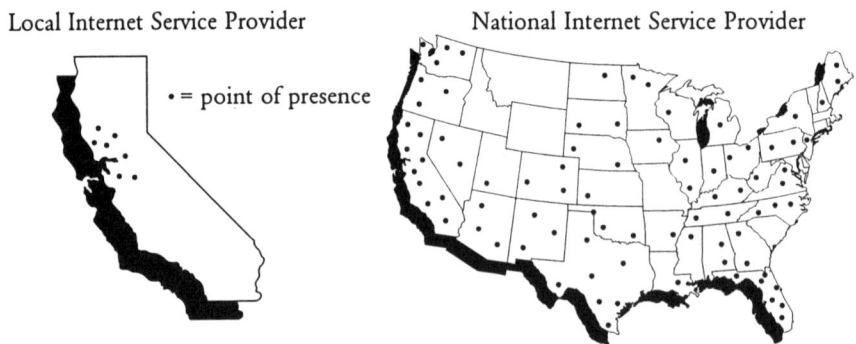

Points of presence are locations where you can get online.

UUNet, you can get online at local phone call rates from Milan, San Francisco, and everywhere else where they have a local access point, or point of presence. Your service provider will give you the details of how to do this. I think it is important for you to know about the portability of your Internet service and e-mail. It is not confined to your computer or even your city.

When I was an America Online member, my computer told my modem to dial a local number in San Francisco where I lived (and still live). When I brought my computer to my parent's home in Greensburg, PA, I found a local number for America Online there and got connected to the Internet with a local telephone call in Greensburg without having to pay for a long distance phone call to San Francisco. I have a friend who did not know this and he bragged to me how neat it was that he could travel all over the the country and get connected to the Internet, just by making a long distance phone call to the same number each time! Knowledge can save you money.

If you are going to be travelling all over the country and getting online in different cities and states, go with a big Internet Service Provider like UUNet, GTE/BBN Planet, or AT&T World Net services, or a Commercial Online Service like Compuserve, Prodigy or AOL so that you don't have to make long distance phone calls to connect to your account. On the other hand, supporting your local community is always nice and personal and if your computer is going to be in just one place, consider your local Internet Service Providers. Call up some local friends and see if they know of any companies with good reputations. *One word of caution: if you get a new computer, it may be configured to automati-*

cally go to one of these services. For reasons which should be obvious ($) it is set up this way, but you can still choose any of the other ways of getting online. One other word of caution: watch out for scams. Terms like lifetime access for a certain fee should scare you. Whose lifetime, yours or theirs?

Don't get too bogged down in the decision though! It's not that tough and once again, everyone is working hard to make this as easy as possible for you. And the good news is that you only have to do this once. If you are really smart, you'll invite your good friend who knows everything about this over for dinner and he or she will set it all up for you. If you are lucky, some computer savy kid will do all the right things so that you can just turn the machine on and it's ready to jump online.

Quick Review

Just to backtrack. We covered what is required to get online. There are several options, from the cheapest (the library) to the more expensive. We looked at the computer, the modem, and the guys on the other end of the phone line, and free e-mail companies too. The choice is up to you. At each step you should be thinking about the three most important words in the computer industry—GOOD CUSTOMER SERVICE. Let other, more experienced people solve your problems. If you get frustrated at any point in the process, relax, take a few deep breaths, and take a short walk. You'll get online—no problem!

OK. Now that we know how to get online, let's venture ahead to the next step, the programs you'll be using.

4

The Big Three: E-mail, The Web, and Usenet

The fates have given mankind a patient soul.
HOMER
C. 700 BCE

Now that you've found a good Internet Service Provider or Commercial Online Service to connect you to the Internet, what do you get for the $20 a month fee? Let's go back to our fitness club analogy. When you join a fitness club you get use of their three main services: the free weights, the running track, and the swimming pool. Each service, while part of the same fitness center, is unique in and of itself: one fitness center, three services. Think of the Internet as a fitness club with three distinct services.

With the Internet, you get e-mail, the Web and **Usenet**. To use e-mail you use a mail program, to use the Web you use a browser, and to use Usenet you use a **newsreader**. While I noted that e-mail stands for electronic mail, and that the Web is full of web sites that look like pages in a magazine which you view with your browser, this is the first time I have brought up Usenet. I'll describe Usenet, or User's Network, in a few moments.

These are the three main Internet services. They are all easy to learn and use. Please do not go out and buy one of those huge, scary books which describes in tedious detail every last option you'll never need to know about these programs. If you spend a little time with each one, everything will fall into place.

Your Internet Service Provider or Commercial Online Service will provide you with the three programs free of charge—an e-mail program, a web browser, and a newsreader. These programs come on the disk or CD-ROM which they send you in the mail. Once again, all three of these programs are free. I'll explain e-mail, then the Web, then Usenet.

In chapters 6, 7, and 8 I cover e-mail, the Web, and Usenet respectively in greater detail. This is just a quick introduction.

E-mail

E-mail, or electronic mail, is quite simply the easiest of all the programs and one of the most powerful communication tools there is. It is awesome. If you could choose just one tool, this is the one to pick. I place it halfway between the letter and the telephone. Why? Because you will be able to communicate with your friends and family all over the world who are also connected to the Internet. You can send and receive messages in minutes. When you use e-mail, you send your letter-like messages to your recipients' computers. In turn, they send messages to you. And you can save these messages for life. Once you start using e-mail, you'll be in contact with friends whom you've never written before and have forgotten to call lately. *It's cheaper than a phone call and ten times easier than writing a real letter.*

The reason it is cheaper than a phone call is that each and every message that you send and receive is free. There are no electronic stamps! Whether you send fifty e-mail messages to your next-door neighbor or a friend in another country, the cost per message is the same. Absolutely nothing. If you are using the free e-mail service, Juno (I talk about these in the previous chapter), there are absolutely no costs. However, as I mentioned in the last chapter, an Internet Service Provider or Commercial Online Service charges a flat monthly rate of around $20 per month for Internet access. This is the monthly membership cost of the club—and you get unlimited use of all the services, of which e-mail is just one. You can send e-mails all over the world at no additional cost beyond the flat monthly fee.

All e-mail programs function the same way, although they come in various shapes and size (just like telephones). If you get connected to the Internet through a Commercial Online Service (see chapter 3), they will provide you with their customized e-mail program. These are usually straightforward and easy to use (although some are better than others). In other words, Compuserve, Prodigy, and America Online all have unique e-mail programs. These come on the floppy disc or CD-ROM they send you.

If you get connected to the Internet through an Internet Service Provider, they will probably provide you with an e-mail program called **Eudora Light**. They will include Eudora Light on the floppy disk or CD-ROM they send you. You can buy the **Eudora Pro** version at your local software store. Eudora (combining the Light and Pro versions) is the most popular e-mail program there is, for both PCs and Macs, and for good reason. The biggest difference between the **Light** and the **Pro** versions is that the Light is free and therefore comes with *no* support, while the Pro has a few extra features and comes with *unlimited* technical support—for all of your questions. The Pro version only costs about $60. I feel that Eudora Light is straightforward and recommend trying it first before buying the Pro version. If you feel you'll need some hand-holding to get through this, go out and buy Eudora Pro for the technical support. Just call them up and ask, "What do this and that and this do?" Their technical support team will take the time to answer each and every one of your questions.

If your Internet Service Provider provides you with a program besides Eudora, give it a shot. If it's easy to use, stick with it. Only switch to Eudora if you have problems, in which case you'll appreciate Eudora's ease-of-use.

The Web

The Web is what you've been hearing a lot about lately. The Web consists of hundreds of thousands of web sites which individuals, professionals, government agencies, organizations, and businesses publish. Web sites look like magazine pages full of text and photographs and stylistic elements. In addition, the Web supports all kinds of other media too such as sound and video. The best part about the Web is that all this information is "linked" together. You can click on words or pictures and these special links will take you to other places. Just as a spider web is connected through the links of thread, the Web is connected by links of information, and that's why it's named the **World Wide Web** or the Web for short. Millions of pieces of information are all strung together for you to access. The Web is a tremendous source of information which will enable you to communicate with people all over the world. Once you use the Web, all of this becomes totally obvious.

To use the Web, you need a browser. Browsers are the viewers of web sites. The browser is what you use to "browse" around the Web and leap from one source of information to another in a single click of your mouse.

Your Internet Service Provider or Commercial Online Service will provide you with 1) **Netscape Navigator**™ or 2) **Internet Explorer**™ or 3) both. You've probably heard of Netscape Navigator™. This is the browser which started the Web revolution. No doubt you've also heard of Microsoft, which has entered the browser market with Internet Explorer™. I highly recommend Netscape partially out of principle because they started the revolution and because their browser is excellent. There is not much difference between the two, so if you have one or the other they'll function in the same way, more or less.

These browsers are free. Your Commercial Online Service or Internet Service Provider will include a browser on the floppy disk or CD-ROM they send you. The e-mail program and the browser come on the *single* disk or CD-ROM which they mail you. So if you were wondering how you get these programs the answer is easy—it comes to you by way of mail. And it's free. Boy, so much free software out there—you do not pay one penny for it!

Usenet Newsgroups

Usenet stands for **User's Network**. It is the hidden gem of the Internet. Usenet is a worldwide system of discussion groups (also described as message boards) covering a myriad of topics such as sports, hobbies, pastimes and on and on. These discussion groups are called **newsgroups** and there are over 16,000 newsgroups presently (more and more are added all the time). Although newsgroups are not nearly as popular as e-mail and the Web, millions of people have found them extremely informative, especially when dealing with an esoteric topic. You can read and post messages to the newsgroups of your choice. Usenet is a worldwide exchange of information (you can think of this as news) in the form of text.

I posted a message about my car for sale in a local Bay Area newsgroup and received phone calls from several people within minutes. If you have a favorite pastime, you are guaranteed to find a newsgroup with thousands of people around the world sharing messages about this particular topic, such as your favorite professional football or basketball team or gardening.

You will use a **newsreader** to access the Usenet discussion groups, or newsgroups. Usenet is simple, like e-mail—just text. It is a special world of its own, a world you just may find extremely beneficial for you. It's hard to give a good description of something so unique and for the most part hidden, because it is not in the spotlight right now. You do not hear about Usenet in the news or see advertisements for it. What this basically means is that there is no money in Usenet, so no hype to surround it. But that does not stop it from being really helpful. In Chapter 8 I will take you through a tour of Usenet by showing you how I use it in a specific situation. This will make it much clearer for you.

Your Internet Service Provider or Commercial Online Service will provide you with a free newsreader program to access Usenet and the newsgroups. This usually comes on the same floppy disk or CD-ROM mentioned above, although sometimes you have to make a special request. Just call up your Internet Service Provider's or Commercial Online Service's customer support and they will either A) send you out a copy on a floppy disk or B) provide you with instructions on how to get it for yourself. There are several newsreader programs. They function in the same way and are, you guessed it, easy to use too.

A Few More Pointers

So now you have the three main tools you need to take care of 99% of your Internet needs: your e-mail program for e-mail, your browser for the Web, and your newsreader for accessing Usenet to read and post messages to newsgroups.

Your Internet Service Provider or Commercial Online Service will give you free versions of each of these on the floppy disk or CD they send you. They will also provide you with directions on how to set up the programs the first time you use them. You will probably have some questions the first time. Here's where a good company with good customer service makes all the difference in the world. The first time that you use these programs requires a few extra steps that you only have to do once. Good technical support can walk you through all the steps and answer your questions too. You do not have to do this by yourself!

You can make your life a lot easier by inviting over a friend who has already done this before to help you set it up. Turn a potentially frustrating time by yourself into an hour or two of bonding with a friend!

Want to know something else? Your web browser is designed to be used as a browser but it also has the additional capability to be used as an e-mail program and a newsreader as well. In other words, you have two ways of accessing e-mail and two ways of accessing Usenet. Some people enjoy using their browser for all of these needs. I prefer to use three separate programs: Eudora for e-mail, Netscape for the Web, and a newsreader called Newswatcher for Usenet. Now you know all of your options.

Moving on...

Up to this point I've avoided explaining in detail how the Internet works because you do not need to know how it works in order to use it. Before I describe in greater detail each Internet service mentioned above, I'd like to answer some of the most popular questions about what the Internet is and how it works.

5

The Internet? The Web? What's the difference?

The most beautiful thing we can experience is the mysterious. It is the source of all true art and science.
ALBERT EINSTEIN
1879–1955

When you are sitting comfortably in front of your computer which is connected to the Internet, and using your programs such as e-mail and your browser, there's a lot going on in the background which you never see. You can happily use the Internet and not have to know a thing about the "mysterious" world on the other end of your phone line. It's like making a phone call—you just dial the number, the phone rings, and suddenly you're talking with your friend in another country. What do you know about the telecommunications system? I certainly don't know too much, yet I use my phone all the time.

The Internet is the same way. You just use your programs and everything else is "transparent" to you. (That is how techies say, "You can't see it.") So, I do not want to confuse you by telling you a bunch of stuff you don't need to know. However, some of it is pretty neat and fairly basic too. At any point, if you are thinking to yourself, "Why do I need to know this?" please, just jump right ahead to the next chapter. This chapter discusses the history and evolution of the Internet and the Web.

Here are a few common questions which you may have asked yourself:
- *What is the Internet?*
- *How does it work?*

- *Who started it and who owns it?*
- *How big is the Internet?*
- *What's the difference between the Internet and the Web?*
- *Why did the Web become so popular?*

Here are the answers to these questions, as well as some extra info which will help give you a good view of the Internet.

In the beginning...

When we say the Internet, we are talking about a worldwide system of computers connected together, the information on those computers, and the people all over the world accessing and sharing that information. No one owns the Internet. People, companies, and organizations just contribute to it the same way that a street fair is full of contributors, but is not owned by any one of them. Let's turn the clock back to 1968, when the Internet began.

When lots of Americans were "turning on, tuning in, and dropping out," a US government agency was worried about designing a system of computers that could communicate with each other in the event of a nuclear war. The United States Department of Defense **A**dvanced **R**esearch **P**roject **A**gency started a project which they named **ARPA**net or **Arpanet**. There's that *net* word again. Back then, and still today, it stands for **network**. A network is simply two or more computers connected together which can talk to one another in their own little computer talk (i.e., digital coding).

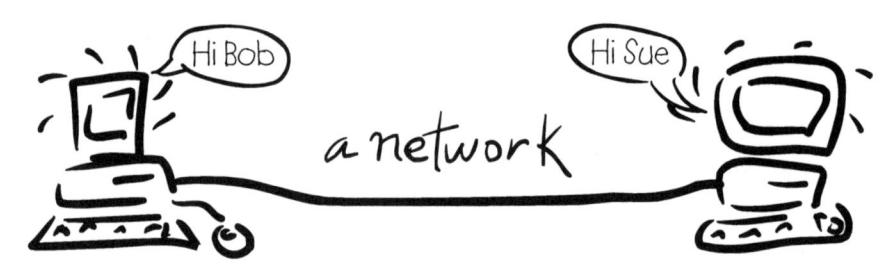

So whether it's two, three, four, ten, or a thousand computers connected together and talking to one another, it's called a network.

Arpanet's initial goal was to design a large scale network across America, from sea to shining sea. It soon became apparent to them that a better goal would be to design a technology that could connect various types of networks into a single large system. So, really, they were designing a technology that allowed individual network pieces to be connected together to make an even larger network.

Legos® and Tinker Toys®

Little kids love building playland villages out of colorful plastic connectable Legos® pieces or wooden structures out of combinable wooden shapes known as Tinker Toys®. When kids grow up they have to play with something else, and what better than computers? People just love putting things together. The folks who were designing Arpanet did a pretty good job of designing a way to connect computer networks together or we would not be mentioning them twenty-nine years later. This concept of an "Internetwork" came to fruition, piece by piece. Internetwork is much too big a word and sounds way too complicated, so they chopped off the "work" part (no one likes work) and voilà, you get the Internet.

As you might imagine, the Internet was really small at first. Just a few networks connected together. You can't create something without giving it a name, so two more really techy words popped up—**LAN** and **WAN**. LAN is just an acronym for **L**ocal **A**rea **N**etwork, while WAN is an acronym for **W**ide **A**rea **N**etwork. When you have a group of computers in one room or one building, connected by cable, the techy folks call this a **Local Area Network**. Now, let's say you have a Local Area Network in San Francisco and one in Pittsburgh. Each is separate and happily operating on its own in isolation. When you connect the two, using high speed phone lines (and one other special piece called a **router** which I'll tell you about next), you have now created a **Wide Area Network**.

LANs, WANs, and Lego® Lands

So, the Internet is a bunch of these LANs and WANs all connected together. (For those who never had the pleasure, Lego® Lands are villages which you create with the colorful connectable plastic Legos® pieces.) There's a magical piece of equipment which allows the techy people to connect these networks together. These are called **routers**. They help find the best *route* from one network to the other. So it's really not that complicated. You start with one computer and then you connect another computer to it. Now you have a network. Add a few more, and you have a bigger network. Toss in more routers, more networks and you have a computer Lego® Land. That's what the Internet is!

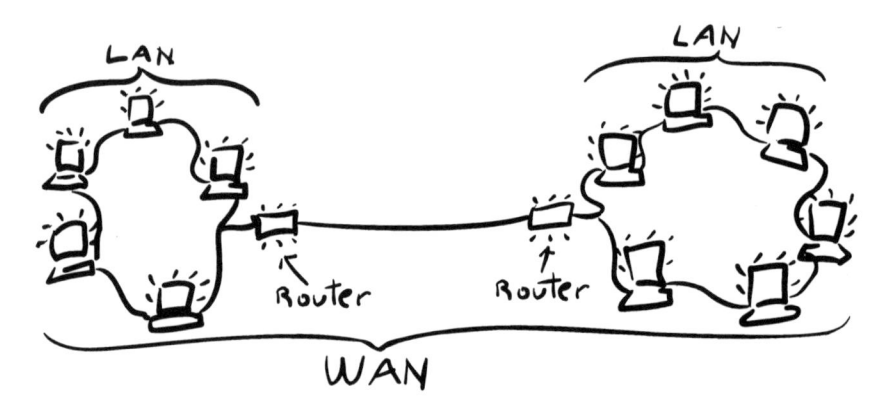

As more and more networks were connected together, a huge demand surfaced for these routers. Today, a company by the name of Cisco Systems has supplied the Internet with 80% of the routers worldwide. With the recent increase in the amount of networks being added, the demand for routers has soared along with Cisco's profitability. In 1996 Cisco was one of the most profitable companies in California.

So if you asked back in the early 1970's how many computers were connected to the Internet, it would be just a few hundred, or maybe a few thousand. The government and universities kept adding more and more computers to this system, even connecting the network to other countries through additional high-speed phone lines and more routers. Nowadays there are hundreds of thousands of computers connected, and more and more are being added each day. Do you see this or feel this? No. It's all the same to you, sitting comfortably at home reading your e-mail and browsing through the Web.

A universal language—but not the language of love

In order to communicate with one another, we must speak the same language. Any two people who have never met can have a conversation if they speak the same language. If both are American, there's a pretty good chance they'll both speak English so they will be able to converse without a problem. In the same way, for all these computers on the Internet to be able to talk to one another, they must speak the same language too.

You will be happy to know that all computers on the Internet do talk to one another in the same language. It is called **TCP/IP**, which stands for, brace yourself, Transmission Control Protocol/Internet Protocol. The reason why I mention this is that you will probably hear the word or see it a few times. It's nothing more than the common Internet computers' way of saying, "Hello, how's it going, here's some information...". A **protocol** is a code (set of rules) which obviously must be agreed upon by those who wish to use it. TCP/IP is the protocol code for communication (transmission) via the Internet.

Pipes of the Internet

Pipes of the Internet

backbone   T3   T1   telephone line

Visual representation of different size Internet cables and lines.

When I said before that the computers of the Internet were all connected together, I left out a little detail about the cables and lines. The cables and telephone lines which connect all the computers of the Internet together are different sizes. Think of these cables and fiber optic lines as pipes. The pipes get smaller and smaller as they stem off from the main pipeline. This main pipeline for the Internet is called the Internet **backbone**. There are actually several backbones owned by the major telephone companies like AT&T, MCI, Sprint, and even a few Internet Service Providers too. The backbones are bridged together in key locations. Stemming from the backbones we have smaller pipes called **T3** and **T1** lines. And finally we have the regular phone lines which then connect to your modem and computer. You'll hear these various terms mentioned. They're just pipes of different sizes.

Another term you'll encounter is **bandwidth**. Bandwidth is the amount of data that can flow through these pipes. The bigger the pipe, the bigger the bandwidth. Think of it in terms of pipes and liquid. Bandwidth is the amount of liquid (data) that can flow through a pipe (cable or phone line).

"Service, please!" demands the client

Now it should be clear that you have networks, routers, a common language, and pipes of various sizes connecting them all together. What more could you want? What does anyone is this world want? SERVICE. That's right. When you go to a restaurant, you would like the waiters and waitresses to serve you. When you go to the bank, you expect good service from the teller. Everywhere we go we want people to serve us, to give us what we want. Well, why expect anything less from this worldwide system of computers called the Internet? When we are at home using our e-mail program, web browser, and newsreader, these programs are called **clients**. Why clients? Because they ask for service, just as we do when we are clients of the restaurants and banks. (*Don't get confused here. When you are using these programs you are not the client, the programs are*). And whom do they ask? Why, the Internet **servers**, of course.

There are lots of these servers on the Internet which give all of your client programs everything they want. Your e-mail program, or **e-mail client**, gets served by **mail servers**; your browser, or **web client**, gets served by **web servers**, and your newsreader, or **news client**, gets served by **news servers**. Just think of these servers as computers on the Internet. When you send an e-mail, your local e-mail program running on your local computer talks to the mail server on the other end of the the phone line. So how does your friend get your message? Your mail server talks to your friend's mail server which delivers the message to your friend's e-mail client.

We're here to serve YOU!

I'm a mail server   *I'm a web server*   *I'm a news server*

The trick to the Internet is that the servers are all really good about communicating with one another. Just as in a restaurant, your waiter or waitress needs to be in communication with the other waiters and waitresses to make sure that all the customers are happily served. They pass messages back and forth to one another all day long. It's no different with Internet servers. Your mail server will send and receive messages to and from other mail servers all over the world, all day long, each and every day of the week, 365 days a year. And you don't even have to tip.

Who owns the Internet?

The response to the question, "Who owns the Internet?" is that no one does. There are lots of computers all over the world with lots of different owners: businesses, universities, government agencies, and so on. They all connect their computers into this system, this world wide street fair of computers and information. There are expenses each step of the way—buying the computers, buying the routers, leasing the high-speed phone lines, setting up the systems, and on and on, but all this is transparent (or invisible) to you. You just click your mouse, and receive.

How about the World Wide Web?

We now know that the Internet is a worldwide system of computer networks. These networks are made up of computers all connected together. Many of the computers are servers such as mail servers, web servers, and news servers. What is the **World Wide Web**? The Web is just one of the Internet services. There are millions of these web servers connected to the Internet. The Internet (the worldwide network of computer networks) can exist and did exist for about twenty years without the Web, just as your fitness club existed for years before they added the new service, the swimming pool. But unlike a swimming pool which can exist independently of a fitness club, the Web cannot exist without the Internet (its infrastructure).

The Web combines the beauty of photographs and pictures (as well as sound, video and much more), with powerful linking abilities so that you can click on the pictures and images and go to other web sites all over the world. You use a browser, which is nothing more than a web client that asks the web servers located throughout the Internet for information, which they gladly serve because that's what they do. The information which web servers serve can be simple text, photographs, music, video—even computer programs—and more.

Who started the World Wide Web?

If you read the first part of this chapter, you learned that the Internet was started by the Department of Defense back in 1968. When did the World Wide Web start and who started it?

A fellow by the name of Tim Berners-Lee had a problem back in 1989. He worked at **CERN**, a particle physics laboratory in Geneva, Switzerland, and was swamped by information. Particles were exploding all over the place, researchers were busy analyzing the essence of subatomic molecules, and information was stacking up and up. Tim and his team were determined to find a better way to deal with all this info. They came up with a hypertext system where documents could be linked together by clicking on words and images. He saw this creation of a "network of links" as a "Web." Hence the name World Wide Web was what they gave to this neat system that they had set up for themselves at CERN. Tim Berners-Lee is commonly referred to as the father of the Web.

A hyper language jumps around

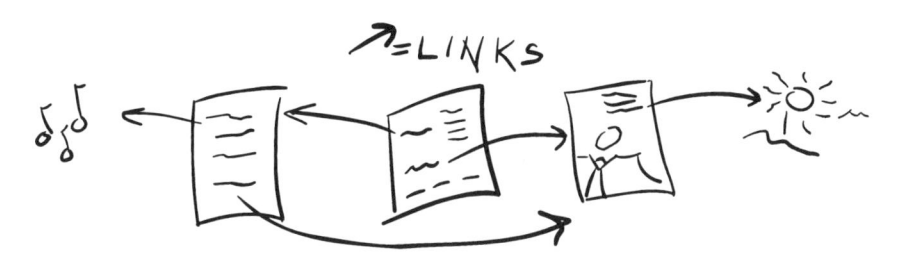

The prefix *hyper* means above. So this hyper text was "above" normal text in the sense that it could do more than regular text. Whereas previously if you saw a reference you would have to go grab another book and look it up, now you could simply click on the word and the reference page appeared. You can just click and immediately jump to the next resource. Tim Berners-Lee created the foundation for the **Hyper Text Transfer Protocol** which is how the web client and the web servers speak to each other (remember, protocol is fancy computer talk for the way computers talk to each other). So when you type in a web address, such as http://www.sunshinedaydream.com, the **http** is referring to this **h**yper **t**ext **t**ransfer **p**rotocol, and **www** to the **W**orld **W**ide **W**eb.

O.K. Cool. The roots of the Internet began in 1968 and the new seed called the World Wide Web wasn't planted until 1989, almost twenty years later. What was going on all that time? Well, not much, as far as you and I are concerned. A bunch of computer people were passing black-and-white text files back and forth through this lattice of computers called the Internet. Pretty bland, if you ask me. However, this new system called the World Wide Web was doing wonders for our friends at CERN in Switzerland, and they thought they would do something really nice—share their invention with the rest of the world.

In January of 1992 they placed the important documentation (the Hyper Text Transfer Protocol) as well as the instructions for creating the web clients (the browser) and the web servers on the Internet—for anyone to access. A programming whiz kid working at the **N**ational **C**enter for **S**uper-Computing **A**pplications (**NCSA**) of the University of Illinois got his hands on this information. He was none other than Marc Andreesen whose team created the first mainstream browser called Mosaic, which was the predecessor to Netscape Navigator™. NCSA released Mosaic versions for Microsoft Windows and the Macintosh. The word got out, people loved it, the visionary Jim Clark envisioned Netscape, he convinced Marc to join him, venture capital poured in, Netscape was formed, Netscape went public, the web revolution began, and the whole world was a better place to live. Something like that, more or less.

A new age of publishing was on the horizon. When you toss together an easy interface, pictures and text, combined with the powerful hypertext linking abilities, why, you're baking quite a pie. When the average person can take a bite, you've got a party. And when people all over the world with important information can all join the same party, without paying too big a price, why, you've got what we call the Web. The World Wide Web has grown by leaps and bounds to be the biggest compilation of information which has ever existed in one accessible place. And with each new web site, sitting on a web server somewhere on the Internet, the Web grows bigger. Anyone can participate in the fair of the Web, as a spectator, an active participant, or just a casual viewer. And while all this information may seem quite intimidating at first, remember that it happened one person, company, and organization at a time.

Taking the Myst out of Mystery

I hope what you just learned took a lot of the "mystery" out of the Internet. Take a little time to think about what we just covered. It's quite a lot of information, I know. Isn't it amazing how all the little pieces fit together?

This may be a good time for a little break. Then we'll take a closer look at the three client programs I mentioned—the e-mail program, the browser and the newsreader—in chapters 6, 7, and 8 respectively.

6

E-mail—Simple, quick, easy, cheap

Dost thou love life? Then do not squander time: for that's the stuff life is made of.
BENJAMIN FRANKLIN
1706–1790

E-mail, or electronic mail, is awesome because it is really easy to use and extremely efficient. After you start using it, you'll find that sending an e-mail to a friend or relative can be easier than giving them a phone call. You don't get a busy signal, you have a permanent copy of your correspondence, and you can send your e-mail anytime, day or night. There are only a few little steps you need to learn, then it's as easy as dialing a telephone number or writing a letter.

I receive e-mails from my seventy-five year old grandfather, old friends from high school, lots of people with whom I work, and countless other acquaintances and close friends and family. Just about everyone sends me e-mail. And I'll bet one of these days I'll get an e-mail message from my parents too! (Actually, after my parents read the final draft of this guide, they purchased a home computer, got online, and did indeed send me an e-mail message. It worked!) In short, every person can use e-mail. It is the universal Internet program.

E-mail borrows several conventions from regular mail (which you may start to call **snail mail** like all of us e-mail enthusiasts). We'll go over these conventions. However, there are no electronic stamps—you do not have to pay for postage. The cost for sending an e-mail from San Francisco to New York City, from San Francisco to Honolulu, and from San Francisco to Tokyo is the same—

absolutely nothing! E-mail messages are free, free, free. *In chapter 4 I explained that the costs involved with getting online usually amount to around $20 per month flat fee. However, if you just want e-mail you can get free e-mail (you avoid the $20 per month Internet connection flat fee but you will not get to use the Web or Usenet) from Juno. Getting connected to the Internet costs money. Sending e-mail is free, free, free. Please jump back to chapter 4 for further details.*

You simply compose your message, point to the e-mail address of the person you're sending the e-mail to, and hit the SEND button in your e-mail program. Off your message goes, bouncing around the Internet until it lands in the electronic e-mail box of the recipient, who then "opens" your message on his or her computer. And unlike regular mail, the entire process requires only a few minutes (even seconds) to get from your computer to theirs after you compose it and press SEND. Pretty amazing when you think about it. And e-mail does not get lost either (well, maybe in Chicago where all US mail gets lost).

E-mail is not nearly as private as regular mail. It is against the law for the regular mail carriers to open your letters and read the contents inside. E-mail does not have such protections. Unfortunately, as a message gets passed from one computer to the next, at any point anyone slightly technical can find a way to read that message. I hope this does not deter you from enjoying this wonderful communication tool. Use it for casual correspondence and everything will be fine.

Starting Out

First, you get online. In the case of the Commercial Online Services (AOL, CompuServe, Prodigy, and MSN) you simply click on their colorful icon which appears on your monitor, get connected, and your e-mail program pops up. With an Internet Service Provider, you'll click on Eudora. Easy enough.

Every e-mail program has the same standard features. There may be a few minor differences, but for the most part the main choices are the same. To compose a letter, you'll choose NEW MESSAGE. (Note: each program will have its own unique look and feel, but the choices are the same. So while one may say

NEW MESSAGE, another may have COMPOSE MESSAGE.) Then you'll see something similar to this:

```
          To:
        From:    Andrew Gold <gold@sunshinedaydream.com>
     Subject:
          Cc:
         Bcc:
X-Attachments:
```

In addition there will be an area for you to put the main text of your letter. We call this the e-mail **body**.

Let's quickly go through each element.

To:

This is the e-mail address of the person to whom you are sending the letter. If you were sending it to me at work, you would put andrew@omix.com. To send an e-mail to your friends and family, you'll need to know their e-mail addresses. How do you get their addresses? Call and ask.

Unlike regular mail, you can send a single message to more than one person. To do this, you create an **address book**. So, if you wanted to create an address book for the kids, you'd find the option to create a NEW ADDRESS BOOK, name it "kids" and then add the e-mail addresses of all your kids to the list. Then, you'd just write:

```
     To:  kids
```

And all of them would receive the same message. Try doing that with regular mail! Similarly, for just a single address, you can create a **nickname**. For instance, by naming a new address book Andrew and putting gold@sunshinedaydream.com in the address list, you will be able to send

41

an e-mail to Andrew rather than having to type the full e-mail address.

And, you can also use a comma to add more than one e-mail address, if you do not feel like creating a new address book.

```
To:   andrew@omix.com, gold@sunshinedaydream.com
```

will send the message to each one of my two e-mail addresses. You can keep going with as many addresses and commas as you like. This little trick comes in handy.

One more quick point—e-mail addresses are **case insensitive**. So, it does not matter whether you use capital or lower case letters. AnDrEw@OMIX.com is the same as andrew@omix.com.

From:

Obvious enough. What is not obvious is that when you open your account, you will need to set up a few things. Then your name and e-mail address will automatically fill in this field. It will save you a few seconds of typing time.

Subject:

When you choose the subject of the e-mail, make sure to be specific. That way, the recipient will be able to know right away what this is concerning. Plus, in the future, when looking through all of your old e-mails, both sent and received, the important message won't be hidden.

Cc:

Cc is an acronym for carbon copy, a relic of the old days when you'd put your letter over a sheet of carbon paper which would produce the carbon copy. Just as with a regular letter, the cc is sent to this e-mail address(es). Same rules apply as with To:

Bcc:

This stands for blind carbon copy. When you cc someone, both they and the other party see this. However, sometimes you want to send an e-mail to someone, but don't want them to know that you are sending a carbon copy to another person. Hence the surreptitious "Bcc." *Note: not all e-mail programs have this feature, although most should.*

X-Attachments:

With e-mail, you can only write simple text in the body of the letter. What happens if you want to send someone a file you have saved on your computer? Well, you would simply attach the file to the e-mail. It's the software version of attaching a document with a paper clip to your letter.

One word of advice: make sure the recipient has the same program you used to create the file you are going to attach to your e-mail. In other words, I created this book in a neat **word processing** program called Claris Works (word processors are programs for composing letters, guides, books, etc.). I named the file *walk w/me.wks*. If I attach this file with my e-mail message and send it to my grandfather for editing, and he does not have Claris Works (or a program which can read Claris Works files), he will not be able to open the attachment.

The E-mail Body

This is the space where you will type in your message. E-mails typically have no fancy formatting which you get with a normal word processor. Normal word processors let you use **bold**, *italic*, underline, *different fonts* and so on. E-mails give you just simple formatting and make `bold, italic, different fonts and so on look like this`. This is the main reason why e-mail is so universal—it is simple and basic.

The Signature

One little extra is the **signature**. You can easily set up your e-mail to automatically include a little area of text where you can add a nice quote, some contact information, or whatever you want. How can you set up your signature? There is no use in me trying to explain since there are simply too many different types of e-mail programs, each with a slightly different way of doing it. My advice: call the technical support line for your Internet Service Provider or Commerical Online Service. They will be able to instruct you on how to do this. Or ask a friend who knows.

Once you receive a few e-mails, you'll get a good idea just how unique and individual this signature can be. Mine looks like this:

```
            a n d r e w   g o l d
         S U N S H I N E   D A Y D R E A M
       - - - http://www.sunshinedaydream.com - - -
    the san francisco bay area outdoor adventure source
```

Ready to send the message

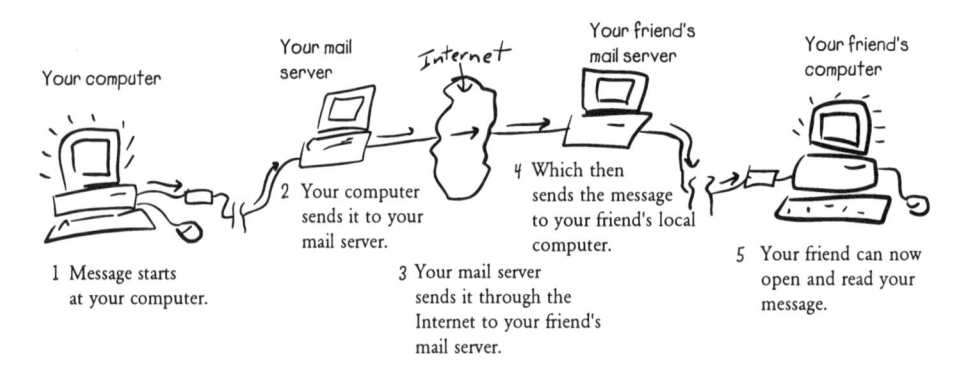

1 Message starts at your computer.
2 Your computer sends it to your mail server.
3 Your mail server sends it through the Internet to your friend's mail server.
4 Which then sends the message to your friend's local computer.
5 Your friend can now open and read your message.

Great! You have filled out the appropriate parts and you hit the SEND button. What happens? Your local e-mail program, that you are using on your computer, talks to the **mail server** on the other end of your phone line. They talk to each other in a catchy term called **Post Office Protocol** or **POP**. "Hey, I've got a message for so and so. Here you go." Your computer sends the e-mail message to the mail server which then transfers your message to the right computer, anywhere on the Internet. Let's take a walk over to the receiving side.

Receiving e-mail

When you open your e-mail program, the very first thing it does is check with the mail server on the other end of your phone line to see if you have received any messages. If so, the nice server transfers them from your account on the server to your local mailbox in your e-mail program. So now the messages physically reside on your computer.

Your inbox will look something like this:

	Who	Date	K	Subject
•	Andrew Gold	11/3/97	3	MacHTTP Software (fwd)
•	money@makealot.com	11/5/97	2	Make money fast!
	QuickTime-VR Digest	11/7/97	17	QuickTime-VR Digest V1 #98
•	mary@pleez.com	11/7/97	5	How's it going?

- The e-mail address or name of the party who sent the message.
- The date on which the message was sent.
- "In" is the name of the Inbox, the mailbox to which new messages come.
- The size (in kilobytes) of the message.
- The subject of the e-mail.
- The dot indicates an unread message while the absence of the dot means that I opened the message and read it.

You just click on the message, it opens up and you read it. One of the nice features you will notice is that all your e-mails come with date and time stamps. This is really helpful when going back over your old e-mails.

Saving your messages to the right folder

Mr. Hutzel, my 7th grade history teacher, would constantly repeat (again and again), "Organization is the key to success." He was right. The trick with e-mail is organization. You can create and name as many new folders as you like for storing your received messages. These computer folders reside on your computer, not the mail server, so you do not have to be connected to the Internet to be able to read your saved messages. Computer folders serve the same function as physical folders. You label them and store information in them. You can create new folders, rename existing ones, remove and/or combine them. You can make a folder for each person who sends you e-mail, or you may prefer bigger chunks like one folder called *Friends* and another called *Family*. At any point you can open the folder and read the saved messages. You can also combine-remove-replace-shuffle the folders too.

People have varying opinions, but I tend to save just about all the messages which come to me from people I know. E-mail messages take up very little space on our computers. Why throw something out when it is so easy to file it away?

Searching through your folders

Your e-mail program will have a special search feature so you can find an e-mail by searching for a word, an e-mail address, the date it was sent, and so on. Basically, you will be able to find any e-mail which you saved. If you threw it out, well, it is gone forever. This is just one more reason why I save anything which is even slightly important.

Replying to a received e-mail

Replying to an e-mail is every bit as easy as sending a new one. If you are lucky, your e-mail program will ask you if you would like to INCLUDE ORIGINAL? which will put the original message sent to you in the body of the e-mail. If it does not ask you to INCLUDE ORIGINAL?, look for this option because it probably exists. If you can not find it, call technical support or ask a friend. You will send plenty of messages and this option is invaluable.

To help distinguish between what you are about to write and what is included, brackets looking like this, >, automatically mark the included text.

Your screen will show the following when you say "Yes" to INCLUDE ORIGINAL:

```
>How's it going?
>Is your new job still a blast?
>Did they fix 19th Avenue yet?
>Still mountain bike riding on Mt. Tam?
```

You can type your reply around the brackets...

```
>How's it going?
```

```
Great!
>Is your new job still a blast?
Yep!
>Did they fix 19th Avenue yet?
Nope. Still has lots of traffic.
>Still mountain bike riding on Mt. Tam?
Every weekend!
```

Most people find this helps save time and prevents any confusion. Imagine receiving this response:

```
Great!
Yep!
Nope. Still has lots of traffic.
Every weekend!
```

Forwarding e-mail messages

If you receive a message and want to pass it on to someone else, you'll choose the FORWARD option. When you forward a physical letter, the only version leaves your possession and goes to the forwarding address. E-mail is different. Here, a copy of the original will remain on your computer, unless of course you decide to throw it out.

There is no privacy. That's right. None.

Be careful what you write in your e-mails because there is no privacy. You can use a program to **encrypt** (to write in a special protected code) your e-mails, but I do not know a single average Internet user who goes to such great lengths. E-mail is great for casual communication, but not a whole lot more. Intimate feelings and trade secrets belong elsewhere. Besides, if you have something really important to say, please put it on physical paper.

The other kind of spam

After you start using e-mail, you will notice more and more random advertising messages filling up your inbox. 90% of the messages I receive are these junk e-mails, commonly referred to as **spam**. The popularity of spam stems from the ability to send millions of e-mail messages for a few dollars.

Spam is really irritating. Just about everyone (besides the spammers who are making $ doing it) despises this incessant barrage of worthless e-mails, sometimes disguised quite nicely. The Coalition Against Unsolicited Commercial E-mail helped draft Representative Chris Smith's anti-spam bill called the Spam Ban. If passed (keep your fingers crossed), the bill would extend penalties already present under the 1991 junk fax law to unsolicited e-mail. The measure has hefty fines which would permit violators to be sued for actual damages of $500 per violation. If this bill is passed, I'm sure we'll all see a lot less of this parasite.

Pretty Cool?

So, that's e-mail in a nutshell for you. Most Internet users casually enjoy sending and receiving e-mails. They'll check their e-mail once every couple of days, or maybe once a week. As soon as you start communicating with your good friends via e-mail, you'll be so glad that you too decided to jump on the e-mail bandwagon. Please do not feel that this will add a huge unnecessary burden to your life. It's actually quite simple, really helpful, and fun. Just ask your friends.

One service down, two to go. Now let's go on to the browser and check out the Web.

7

Browsing the Web

*Life that dares send,
A challenge to his end,
And when it comes, say, welcome friend!*
RICHARD CRASHAW
1613–1643

Remember how easy everything was when you were a kid? You would just play all day without any worries. Life just danced along until you hit a time of great turmoil—puberty. Then, the hormones inside your body were fighting hard to change your cells, your body structure, and your formation into an adult. Growing pains were a part of our lives.

Well, right now the Web is going through some growing pains too, especially in the area of the browser. You see, since 1992 when Tim Berners-Lee released the blueprints for a browser to the world, it has been a nonstop struggle to improve and redefine the way the browser works. Netscape came first and showed the world just how neat the Web looked through its browser. There was Netscape Navigator™ version 1, then version 2, then version 3 and now version 4. On the other side, we have Microsoft which abruptly entered the browser market with Internet Explorer™. They too went through a couple of versions, almost in synch with Netscape. It's a challenge knowing which is the right browser, the right version of the right browser, and what else you need.

Browser puberty

Why I am I telling you all this? To expose the real source of the confusion—BROWSER PUBERTY. You may wonder which browser is better and why some companies support Netscape while others support Microsoft. You'll see signs saying, "This web site best viewed with Netscape Navigator™ 4," when you only have Navigator™ 3. America Online may default to Internet Explorer™, although you would prefer Netscape Navigator™. Why can't the world be simple? Because there is no money in simplicity. At least, not on the Web.

Netscape Navigator™ vs. Microsoft Internet Explorer™

Netscape used to have about 90% of the worldwide browser market share, then in 1996 it decreased to 70%. Why? Because at that time Microsoft brought out Internet Explorer™ and paid a lot of money to strategic partners who helped push their new toy. Whether bundling it with Windows 95®, paying America Online a fee to make their browser the default selection or paying Apple Computers $150 million dollars to make Internet Explorer™ the default browser selection on all new Macintosh computers, Microsoft is doing everything it can to steal Netscape's momentum and market share. How do I feel about this? I think competition is great for the consumer, you and me. However, Microsoft has a bad habit of putting the competition out of business, which abruptly ends all competition. And then we all know what happens next. We, the consumers with no options, pay the price.

I, like many other participants of the Web, believe it was Netscape who had the vision and their products really reflect their dedication to advancing the Web.

The good news is that both browsers have the same "look and feel," so going between the two will be easy enough. With this said, let's talk about some of the basic features.

Hyper Text—the Hyper Language

The Web is a series of web pages which you can see by clicking on words, pictures, or typing in a **URL**. URL, which stands for Uniform Resource Locator, is simply a web address. When I say go to http://www.sunshinedaydream.com, I just gave you the URL of my site. I do not like this term and prefer to say web address which is a lot less techy. The **http** is an acronym (no shortage of these in the computer world) for **hyper text transfer protocol**, which is the language the web servers and web browsers speak to each other. The neatest thing of all is that documents all over the world can link to each other in a million ways. Once you start clicking around, you'll get the hang of it.

The actual web pages are written in **HTML** or **Hyper Text Markup Language**. This is just a special formatting language which tells the browser how the page should look, where the images should go, what color the text should be, and so on. Because the browsers have the power of interpretation, the same web page can look drastically different in two different browsers. Another relic of browser puberty. You may notice lots of files ending in **.html** or **.htm**. This is a standard suffix for web pages written in HTML. HTML, by the way, is fairly simple in its most basic form. That's why you'll find so many teenagers playing around with it.

The Missing Link: DNS

How do computers on the Internet find each other? This is a good question. I am going to give you a brief explanation. I could have brought this up in an earlier chapter, but this seems like a great place for this description. If this gets confusing, simply browse over the next few paragraphs.

Let's start with a concept familiar to everyone, mail addresses. You can mail a letter to most places in the world using a mail address. Computers on the Internet have addresses too. These Internet addresses are called **domain names**. A domain name identifies a unique computer on the Internet in the same way that a mail address identifies a unique location.

In the United States, mail addresses have a standard format. Our name goes on the first line, our street address (or P.O. Box) next, which is followed by our city, state, and zip code. US post offices have a system that enables them to find the correct address using this information. Internet addresses, or domain names as they are technically called, have a special format too. They come in the form of two or more names separated by . characters (periods). The domain name sunshinedaydream.com is an address for an Internet computer. Don't get confused here—these are just definitions! This will make much more sense in moment.

telephone number = 415.123.4567

IP address = 206.40.77.207

In chapter 5, I explained how computer networks are similar to telephone networks. We all know how to pinpoint a location anywhere in the United States using just a number. We simply pick up a telephone and then dial the telephone number. It's easy to use a number to pinpoint a location, or a device anywhere in the world. The computers on the Internet use numbers too. Only these are not called telephone numbers (which are only for telephones!) but rather Internet computer numbers. The techy folks call these Internet computer numbers, **IP addresses.** (The **IP** stands for Internet Protocol, but you do not need to know this.) It's called an IP address, but it is really a number.

domain name ⇄ DNS ⇄ **IP address**
(sunshinedaydream.com)   (206.40.77.207)

The Domain Name System, or DNS, translates domain names into IP addresses and vice versa.

The missing link is the special system which translates a domain name, such as sunshinedaydream.com, into an IP address (Internet computer number). Am I saying that sunshinedaydream.com gets translated into a totally bland number? Yes! The name of this special system that does this is called the **Domain Name System.** The Domain Name System, or **DNS**, translates domain names into IP addresses (and vice versa). All domain names, such as sunshinedaydream.com, omix.com, netscape.com, aol.com, etc., get translated into their unique IP addresses by the Domain Name System. (There are actual computers called **DNS servers** which do all of the translation.)

What does an IP address look like? The IP address for sunshinedaydream.com is 206.40.77.207. An IP address is nothing more than a number which identifies each and every computer on the Internet. No two IP addresses are the same just as no two telephone numbers are the same.

I hope this helped to fill in the missing link—how all the computers on the Internet find each other. It's the exact same system for e-mail too. A domain name, such as aol.com, or w3.org, or any of the Internet domain names gets translated into an IP address which is nothing more than a computer number. And, the routers which I talked about before are very good at locating the right computers using these numbers. Routers route information to the right IP address.

The Top-Level Domains

While we are on the subject of domains, you may have seen these before. Here's what they stand for:

.com	commercial organizations or miscellaneous
.edu	educational institution
.gov	government
.int	international organization
.mil	military
.net	networking organization
.org	non-commercial organization

These are the 7 **top-level organizational domains**. The **top-level domain** is the most general part of the domain. In gold@sunshinedaydream.com, the .com is the top-level domain. And, the **organizational** reference simply comes from the kind of organization we are talking about, as noted above. In the future, you will see .info, .arts, .firm, .web, .store and several more as well.

There are also country domains called **geographical domains**. These two letter abbreviations indicate the country of origin.

In the domain gilbertogil.com.br, the br stands for Brazil. Here are a few of the more common **geographical domains**:

.ar	Argentina
.au	Australia
.br	Brazil
.ca	Canada
.de	Germany("Deutschland")
.es	Spain("España")
.fr	France
.gb	Great Britain
.hk	Hong Kong
.il	Israel
.it	Italy
.jp	Japan
.mx	Mexico
.nz	New Zealand
.su	Soviet Union
.tw	Taiwan
.uk	United Kingdom
.us	United States
.ve	Venezuela

Every once in a while an article appears about someone selling a domain for an exorbitant amount of money. This is called **cybersquatting**. A good domain is worth money because it is easy to remember. How did they reserve those domains? They filled out a form at the **InterNIC**, the **I**nternet **N**ames **I**nformation **C**enter, a special agency in charge of Internet domain names. When you see an ad for a web site, it's the domain name you need to remember. Just one more element of hype in this day and age of the Web. "You gotta have a really catchy web site name!"

The World Wide Wait

The World Wide Web has often been labeled the "world wide wait" due to the delays which you will experience **downloading** all those colorful pictures, graphics, and multimedia elements which make the Web so much fun. Downloading is transferring files from another computer to your computer. There are several factors which cause delays. From a slow modem to a slow web server, to too much Internet traffic (the pipes fill up), there is no shortage of obstacles. Patience is a virtue and waiting is a part of the Web. Please don't get me wrong; it's not that bad. Well, some web sites are really bad, but if they are designed properly, you won't even notice. Or, I should say, you won't notice as much.

Some Common Browser Features

The Web is really hard to describe. You have to see the web sites and click on the links to get a good idea of how hyper text works. All this technical stuff which I am telling you is irrelevant when it comes to using the browser. You just click and click and click and your browser and the mysterious system on the other end of the phone line does the rest. There are a few features about a browser which are worth pointing out, and these will pretty much remain the same, just as your hair and eyes kept their same color during your puberty years.

The HOME BUTTON

Each and every time you start your browser, it will automatically go to a web site. We call this site **home** and there is a HOME BUTTON you can press which will take you back there. You can change the default home selection to whichever site you like. I have my HOME BUTTON set to http://www.sunshinedaydream.com, so this is always the first site I see upon launching my browser. *On a side note, people and companies commonly refer to their web site as their* **home page**. You can set your HOME BUTTON to your favorite web site which hopefully will be Sunshine Daydream too (direct marketing 101).

The URL Window

> You may be wondering, "How do I tell the browser to go to a web site such as http://www.sunshinedaydream.com?" You should see a little window in your browser which displays the web address of your current location. Just type the web address where you want to go in this window. You can type over the current web address and then press ENTER and your browser will go to the new location.

Ability to change letter size (this is called font size)

> If you have trouble reading all the little print, you can change the size of the letters (or font) to your liking. This is a really helpful feature especially if you are sore from having to strain your eyes and neck reading that tiny text.

BOOKMARKS

> As you are jumping around the Internet, leaping from one web page to another, you will find some particularly helpful web pages which you want to make easily accessible to yourself. Browsers have a BOOKMARK feature which lets you add the URL to your **Bookmark List**. Then, when you want to go to that site, your browser just goes right to that web page identified by its URL.

The GO Menu

> There is a GO menu which allows you to see the path of all the locations you have visited from your most recent browser session. As you visit a new page, it adds it to your "history" list. Each click or web address which you type adds to the list. At the end of the session, you can look at the list and see each and every place that you visited. But this will go away whenever you close your browser.

BACK and FORWARD Buttons

> The BACK and FORWARD buttons (these may be little arrows too)

do nothing more than climb up and down your "history" list mentioned above. These buttons work in a sequential manner.

Extra storage space for web files

Because the information coming across the Internet takes time to get from their web server to your web browser, web browsers try to save some of this information locally on your computer. Obviously by being on your computer your browser does not need to download (transfer files to your computer) this information again and therefore the next time you reference the web page, it pops up right away. The fancy word for this storage area for text, pictures, and sounds is disk **cache**. You can increase or decrease your cache depending on how much extra space you have on your hard disk.

The STOP Button

This stops the web page from loading in full. You'll use this one a bunch. When you go to a web site and the images and text start popping up on your screen, you may find out right away that you aren't interested in this particular site. Rather than wait the two or three minutes to have the web page load in full, you just hit STOP. The page stops loading, and then you are free to go somewhere else.

A word about plug-ins

As if the browser battle was not enough, you're just going to love to hear this: browsers have missing parts. That's right. You will go to web sites and they'll have some special video to see, or game to play, which you will not be able to see with your browser alone. They'll inform you that you need to get special parts called **plug-ins** which "plug into" your browser for additional functionality.

These web sites will direct you to another web site where you will be able to download the special piece of software that they want you to get. These plug-ins can be pretty big which means they take a while to download. This is a good time to go for a quick walk or jog or make a phone call or hurt your eyes watching the little download percentage meter on your computer screen.

Some of the most popular plug-ins are the *Real Audio* and *Real Video* plug-ins which enable you to hear and see audio and video respectively without a long delay. A cool company in San Francisco called Macromedia (I ride my bike past their building on 4th and Townsend on my way to the commuter train) makes a few versions of the *Shockwave* plug-in for animations and interactivity. Apple Computer makes a *Quick Time VR* plug-in for seeing incredible 360 degree pictures on the Internet. Sunshine Daydream has a whole section of around fifty of these panoramas shot throughout the city of San Francisco. When you go to this portion of Sunshine Daydream, we have instructions on what you need and where to get it.

There are hundreds, even thousands of these plug-ins. Each company with their own software products can adapt these to the Web and create a special plug-in. Plug-in puberty! I have to admit that it is intimidating and confusing at times. Download a plug-in only when you are really intrigued. If not, just don't download it and move on.

Moving Along...

Chapters 9 and 10 are devoted to taking a closer look at the Web. In this chapter I explained some of the main concepts behind the browser and how it works. We looked at Internet domain names, IP addresses, and the Domain Name System as well. The browser itself is as easy as can be to use. It's all the hype and competition surrounding the browser, not the browser itself, which is hard to handle.

We've covered e-mail. We've covered the Web. Now let's go to Usenet newsgroups. You may be unfamiliar with Usenet because it's low key. No hype. Just good old fashion discussion groups/message boards about everything.

8

Newsgroups—The Hidden Gem of the Internet

Lost, yesterday, somewhere between sunrise and sunset,
two golden hours,
each set with sixty diamond minutes.
No reward is offered, for they are gone forever.
HORACE MANN
1796–1859

Usenet stands for User's Network and it is a worldwide system (isn't everything on the Internet worldwide?) of discussion groups (or message boards, if you prefer this term). It is a unique Internet service which is distinct from both the Web and e-mail. As I said before, it is a hidden gem.

Let me give you a walk through of how I use Usenet so that you can gain a much better idea of what it is and why you would enjoy using it too.

First of all, to access Usenet you will use a newsreader program. Your Internet Service Provider or Commercial Online Service should provide you with the newsreader program on the floppy disk or CD which they send you. If you do not have the newsreader program, call the customer support number of your service and ask them to send you a newsreader program or instruct you where you can get a newsreader program for yourself. They will also be able to inform you how to set up your newsreader which takes about two minutes (if all goes smoothly). I have said it before and will say it again, good customer service and technical support will make your life much easier.

With this said, let's journey through Usenet...

Finding people or groups with your same interest

I live in San Francisco and ride my bike to Caltrain, the public commuter train, which I take to Redwood City. Caltrain allows bicycles on the trains, however there is a shortage of bike space and several commuters and riders with bicycles are turned down. They usually end up taking the next train (if it too isn't full). It's a real bummer. I personally have encountered full trains on several occasions and have written to Caltrain to express my concern. Today I thought I'd go and see if anyone else is concerned too or if anyone in the Bay Area has proposed any solutions to this problem.

I clicked on my newsreader program. This **news client** will talk to the **news server**. The very first thing it does is pull up the FULL GROUP LIST. This list has over 16,000 different groups arranged in alphabetical order. There is an amazing variety of different news groups out there. Each group is focused on a particular topic. This huge system evolved from a small electronic bulletin board started in 1979 at the University of North Carolina. Another case of something small catching a big breeze of participation and growing wildly beyond the creators' imagination.

I happen to know that the Bay Area groups start with ba. The first time I started using Usenet I had no idea what the list meant. As you play around a little, the list starts to make more and more sense. It is definitely worth a few minutes to scroll down the whole list too. The abundance of sex sites tends to draw attention to the wandering eye. The Full Group List that I am seeing does not include all the news groups in the world. Some are regional and local while others are truly global. From personal experience I know that the San Francisco Bay Area has a nice section, and I scroll down to the ba part.

On the way down the list, I pass a huge section starting with alt.sex.fetish. After fetish, arranged alphabetically are words like feet, jello, panties, tickling, wrestling, and a whole lot more. But I just want to go to the Bay Area newsgroups so I scroll down and down. I pass a section alt.sports followed by different sports' names as well as team names too from college basketball to all of the professional football teams. Finally I scroll down to ba.announce, the first Bay Area newsgroup.

What's inside each newsgroup?

Here's part of the list for the Bay Area:

```
ba.announce
ba.bicycles
ba.broadcast
ba.consumers
ba.dance
ba.food
ba.forsale
ba.general
ba.helping-hand
ba.housing
ba.Internet
ba.Internet.media-coverage
ba.israelis
ba.jobs.agency
```

When I double click on the newsgroup ba.forsale, the news server sends data to my local news program which is a list of all the **articles** in this newsgroup. The articles are postings from people around the Bay Area and responses to those postings. Some newsgroups have a few articles inside, while others have over 500 articles. This evening there are 541 articles in ba.forsale which is usually pretty popular. People post all kinds of goods which they are selling. It looks a lot like e-mail and you see the name of the person who posted the message as well as the subject. When you double click on the bar with this information, the full message opens up and you can read the contents inside. The entire Usenet system works this way. You just need to see how one part works, then the rest follows. It is a giant series of repetitions.

About a year ago I sold my Honda Prelude. I didn't feel like paying money to put a classified ad in the paper. Instead, I bought a For Sale sign and taped it on my car window and I also posted a message in ba.forsale. I received more phone calls from interested folks who saw my message in the newsgroup than from those who saw the sign on the car. Granted, the Bay Area does have the largest concentration of people on the Internet in the entire world.

Usenet is *free*. Anyone can post an article to any group. Lots of people enjoy Usenet because it is so simple and easy, and it does not change. It looks the same as it did fifteen years ago. I wasn't online then, but these old giants don't change much. It's not the nature of the beast. That's what makes Usenet so nice too. It's a relic of the way life was before the advent of all the sounds, pictures, and videos on the Web.

Going into ba.bicycles

When I click on the newsgroup, ba.bicycles, a message comes up telling me that it's retrieving the list of **subjects** and **authors**. An author is simply a person who composes a message and posts it to the newsgroup and their topic is the subject. Today there are 465 articles chronologically arranged from oldest to most recent at the bottom. There are also indications of how many **replies** the postings received. In one case, a person posted an article with the subject I Hate Bay Area Traffic! and to the far left a little triangle points to the number 69. That means that there are sixty-nine replies to that article which appear in consecutive order under it. If I click on the triangle, all sixty-nine replies appear. And you can read one, all, or none of these or any of the other articles.

As I click on the articles and open them up, a little counter at the top indicates the total number of articles in this group and keeps track of the number of opened ones.

I could easily do a SEARCH for "Caltrain" and it would take me right to any article with Caltrain in the subject, but I enjoy seeing all of the various other subjects too. I see a few postings about the 1997 Bart strike, and also the nationally famous Critical Mass. As I go down the list, I see a few articles that concerned folks have posted in regards to Caltrain. One which catches my attention is an article with the subject: Caltrain to add another bike car—heard on npr. A nice guy posted this message with the number to call to show support for adding another bicycle train. I see the number 2 to the far left meaning there are two messages for this post. The original and one reply. I click on the triangle to the left in order to access the one reply. I double click on the reply article. It is from a woman who called the number that the man had posted. It turns out that NPR made a mistake on the radio show, and she learned that the number was wrong. She posted the right number to call as well as her little adventure in obtaining it.

Posting your own messages and replying

To post a message or reply to one of the other messages, you choose the appropriate button. You can CREATE NEW or REPLY to an existing article. You have one line for your subject and a big blank area for your message body which is the main content of your posting. This can be one paragraph or twenty pages. Usually short and concise messages make the strongest point. And just like e-mail, there is no special formatting such as **bold**, *italic*, underline, *different fonts* and so on. `Bold, italic, underline, and different fonts look like this.`

First you'll compose your message, fill in the subject line, then hit POST. This sends it to the news server which will update your message locally, then tell all the other news servers throughout the world to update their articles. Like good friends, they are constantly communicating with one another and sharing all their new articles within all the various newsgroups. The worldwide updating process can take a few days to a few weeks. So while your new article may appear right away locally, it may take a week to show up in Japan. In the case of the Bay Area newsgroup, it may just be local anyway so it does not have this problem. An international newsgroup, like news.newuser, which is the place to go for questions about Usenet, may encounter this delay.

Also, you can post the same message to more than one newsgroup at the same time. Just as with e-mail in which you can send the same e-mail message to several recipients, your newsreader program will have an option to send the same posting to more than one newsgroup. How do you do this? Your newsreader program will have the option somewhere. Need help? Call a knowledgeable friend or technical support.

Subscribing and Unsubscribing

For this last example I needed to scroll down the FULL GROUP LIST to find the groups of interest to me. I could save myself a little time by **subscribing** to just

63

the newsgroups I wanted to read. That way, I wouldn't have to scroll through 16,000 newsgroups just to get to the few that I want. While newspapers do have subscription fees, newsgroups do not. To subscribe to a newsgroup, I drag the group that I want into my **Subscription Group Window**. Likewise, if I do not want to read any of the articles of a particular group, I'll pull it out of my Subscription Group Window and this will automatically **unsubscribe** me.

If you know ahead of time of a good newsgroup that you want to see right away, just use the keyword SEARCH feature. You type in the newsgroup name and hit FIND and it will take you right there if it exists.

A View from Above

I thought this view of the Usenet might be helpful in characterizing the functionality and personality of newsgroups. I could go into much more detail about how the system works, but by now you've probably started to realize that all these services on the Internet work in more or less the same way. The computers share information with one another and because they all speak the same language, it's pretty standard. Usenet is clearly different from e-mail and the Web, but the whole communication thing is the same. Usenet is all text which makes it much less visually "exciting" than the Web. However, people's stories, opinions, suggestions, and advice can be really engaging, provocative, and entertaining too. You'll have to be the one who decides if there is anything out there for you on Usenet. With more than 16,000 topics of interest, there's a good chance you will.

A few bits of Usenet advice

Get the FAQs.

FAQ stands for Frequently Asked Questions. It is pronounced like "fact." A FAQ is a compilation of the most common questions and answers to those questions. This is a good place to start for the majority of your questions. Where do you find these? You will see various articles in newsgroups with the subject mentioning the word FAQ. An article subject may be entitled: `Bay Area Bicycles FAQ` in which case I can probably start here with any questions that I have about this particular newsgroup. As you use Usenet, you'll see lots of such articles mentioning the word FAQ. Some FAQs will be helpful, other won't.

Moderated vs. Unmoderated Newsgroups

Some newsgroups are **moderated**, meaning someone volunteers their time to read through all the postings and decides which ones are right for the group and which ones are better for the trash. Your postings and replies go to the **moderator** rather than directly to the newsgroup. On the whole, moderated groups have a much higher quality of content, since the **unmoderated** groups are open game for any and all. With unmoderated newsgroups, there is no one preventing postings, no matter how unrelated to the topic of the newsgroup.

Creating a new newsgroup.

There is a simple procedure for starting a new newsgroup. I figure if you are that proficient, you will have made contact with a person who can direct you to the right place. `news.newgroup` is a good place to start.

A word of caution

Sometimes you wonder just how much time certain people spend online using some of these services. Usenet is one prime example. There are entire communities of Usenet users who establish these silly rules which they relentlessly enforce. If you make a little mistake, they will send you really detailed e-mails informing you just how wrong you were. There is no shortage of people who know twice as much as you and want to impress you with their knowledge. Please do yourself a favor—take these folks with a grain of salt. They are trying to be helpful, but can quickly cross the line to rude. They are in the minority and please don't let them discourage you.

One other word of caution: always think twice before posting a message when you are mad or frustrated. You will see various messages posted by angry folks. When they attack companies, organizations, or people, there is usually a retaliation. These retaliations in the form of postings and e-mails are called **flames** because they burn in the spiritual sense. The last thing you want is to be involved in a bitter conflict with people all over the world. Sometimes by being anonymous we can lose our sense of control and decency. We would never say such things to someone in person or to someone we actually know that we write in moments of frustration or exasperation. Here's a bit of advice from a good friend, "Take two days and think about it before posting anything when angry."

Usenet is there when you need it.

Have fun with this neat connection tool. There's a topic for everyone in Usenet. And if it isn't there, you can easily create it. I usually drop in a newsgroup every once in a while. Maybe once every couple of weeks or months, or when I am looking for something in particular. Usenet is that tool that comes in really handy when you need it, but it's certainly not the most used one in the shed. Like all helpful tools, it's good to know how to use it, especially when it makes your life easier.

Wow! We covered all three major Internet services. Congratulations! We just have a few pages left. Let's go take a closer look at the Web...

9

Finding everything you're looking for: The Search Engines

Attempt the end, and never stand to doubt;
Nothing's so hard but search will find out.
ROBERT HERRICK
1591–1674

Please don't waste your money buying books that help you find what you need on the Internet. These references, such as the *Internet Yellow Pages*, are outdated the second they go into print. The best references on the Internet are the main search engines. Search engines provide directory services and organize the information on the Web into categories to help you easily find what you are looking for. Think of them as the card catalogs for the Internet. The main ones, such as Yahoo (http://www.yahoo.com), Excite (http://www.excite.com), Infoseek (http://www.infoseek.com), Lycos (http://www.lycos.com) and a few more you will come to know eventually will serve the majority of your needs if you're like most folks on the Web.

You'll be glad to know that they are free to use. How do you use them? Open your web browser and enter one of the web addresses listed above. Netscape Communicator™ (as well as most other browsers) automatically includes links to the most popular search engines in its BOOKMARK LIST.

With the search engines you enter the name of the subject or title for which you are searching into a little box. Then you hit "FIND" or some such button.

The search engines sort through their large databases of information and return a list of sites which match your criteria. Depending on what you're looking for they may find zero to tens of thousands of resources. You have to just do it and then you'll get the hang of what's going on. I just went to Yahoo and searched for the word Internet. It found 31777 site matches. Way too broad. But I really just wanted to know about the history of the Internet, so I typed in, "history of the Internet" and now it finds 290 site matches. This is much more manageable.

The search engines make their money from advertising. When you type in your search criteria, they give you the results of your find as well as advertisements which pertain to your area of interest. This is extremely strategic advertising. Search on golf and you get golf ads, computers and computer ads. Right now the majority of search engines are losing money. They are hoping to find revenue sources as they become familiar brand names, but this has yet to be seen. I like them because they are, in this order, *free* and *useful*.

Additional features

In addition to finding web sites (and even Usenet articles and e-mail addresses of people and companies), they offer special services for Road Maps, Driving Directions, Internet Yellow Pages, Stocks, Weather, and more. In short, they are hoping to cover all of your needs under one roof. Search engines soon become a familiar friend.

The Maps/Driving Directions are particularly impressive. You can enter any street address in the United States (and even other countries too) and a map will pop up with an X marking your specified location. You can zoom in and out on the maps and move around in all directions. In addition to marking the spot, you can click on Driving Directions. You'll enter your departure address and the smart computer will connect the roads you can take to get there. Granted, this is all fairly robotic so it doesn't know the short cuts, but it is surprisingly powerful, accurate, and detailed. The smart computer will give street names and exact distances. No more getting lost for you!

Hand-made in the USA

Of all these search engines, Yahoo! is special. Two Stanford students, Jerry Wang and David Filo, started Yahoo! back when the Web was sprouting in 1994. They organized all the new web sites into categories and lists which everyone else could use. They would browse around the Web, and organize all the sites they saw into categories and lists. When they began doing this, the Web was small. There were only a few hundred then a few thousand web sites. As the Web expanded, Yahoo! grew with it and the two guys hired a team to organize the sites by hand, just as they had done in the beginning.

The Yahoo! of today is a multi-billion dollar publicaly-traded company which holds the most complete hand-organized list of web sites around. In addition to these lists, and the other neat services which just about all the search engines have in common, Yahoo! is creating metro sites which are miniature Yahoos! for various cities. When I am looking for web sites in the Bay Area, I go to Yahoo!'s SFBay site. I find that Yahoo! serves most of my needs, although sometimes I use Excite and occasionally the other ones too. But Yahoo! is unique. And what a great name!

Special Search Tricks

Each engine has a special page for advanced searching options. If you are having trouble finding too many web sites or not enough, I suggest taking this next step. Somehow this feature eludes many, but hopefully not you. Like riding a bike, the more you do it the easier it gets. Where do you find this option? They advertise it, usually right next to the little box where you enter the subject for which you are searching. You'll see a little sign for "Search Options," or "Special Search Tricks." Their directions are usually clear.

Who enters all this information in the search engines?

Search engines have large **databases** of information. A database is a program which stores information and optimizes it for quick retrieval. How did all the information get into these databases? Yahoo! is special in the sense that most of its content is entered by hand, by actual living and breathing Yahoo! employees. The other search engines have special programs called robots which click around the Web from site to site. The robots are trained (or programmed) to add each site to their databases and to index the words of the sites too. These robots are constantly traversing the Web, checking, adding, and revising the information they store about millions and millions of web pages.

With Sunshine Daydream, I submitted my site to Yahoo! SFBay and a few days later I received an e-mail from an actual person there who informed me that my site was now appearing in Yahoo! SFBay. Several of the other search engines find Sunshine Daydream too because their robots picked it up. (Another behind-the-scenes insight for you.)

A quick word about these huge warehouses of information

The word database is becoming much more common. What does a database do? Databases are huge data reservoirs which can sort and organize pretty much anything and everything we call information, whether text, images, sounds, videos, movies, or numbers. Databases are the key to all these search engines and services which give you the power to find what you want. Searching through hundreds of millions of articles is a staggering task, but these robust databases perform queries in a matter of seconds.

You might imagine then that because databases are so critical to the whole information structure there are big $$ in it. You are correct. Oracle is the second largest software company in the world (behind Microsoft) and their specialty is the database. I see their five huge glass cylinder buildings from the train car as it goes through San Carlos. The second and third largest database companies, Sybase and Informix respectively, also have useful ways to deal with millions of pounds of raw data.

So that's the search engines in a nutshell. Let's jump over to the last big part, the heart and soul of the Web...

10

The Heart and Soul of the Web

I carry the sun in a golden cup,
The moon in a silver bag.
WILLIAM BUTLER YEATS
1865–1939

The Web is what the Web is. Who's to say what's the leg, the trunk, or the whole elephant? I personally see the benefit of the Web in the way we use it. One thing is for sure, when you use the Web, you are in control. From this perspective, I see three main spheres which are interwoven:

❶ Connecting to the Global Village. From researching companies to looking for a job to finding recipes to joining an online community, the world comes a little closer.

❷ Dissemination of traditional big media information such as news, stocks, weather, newspapers, classified sections, radio stations online, and so on.

❸ A Powerful Distribution/Commerce Tool. Shop, shop, shop. Buy, buy, buy.

Sphere 1: Connecting to the Global Village

There are millions and millions of these web sites, or **home pages** as some refer to them, and thousands are created each day. Are you going to spend all of your time just "surfing" around the Web day after day? I surely hope not. I don't and I do not know anyone who does. Most of the time you will use the Web to find a helpful bit of info which interests you.

Whether it is a class reunion web site, a site for your favorite place to vacation, or a special recipe for sticky rice with mangos, the Web brings you closer to people, places, and ideas. Want to know something about a particular company? No more having to search through the library. The Web reflects the general interests of the entire world. The sights and sounds of the world are just a few clicks away.

Unfortunately, this includes the bad as well as the good. Hate, prejudice, ignorance, anti-semitism, and racism have a new voice for spreading their harmful messages. Freedom of speech has a new test in the day and age of the Web.

I don't want to waste your time by going over all the obvious resources on the Web. You'll find them for yourself (probably using the search engines). There are, however, a few areas of interest I'd like to toss into the spotlight.

Sex and the Web

You've probably heard a lot about pornography and the Internet. On June 26, 1997, the Supreme Court of the United States of America (No. 96-511) ruled that a new law barring indecent material from the Internet cannot be enforced because it violates free-speech protections and is unconstitutionally vague. The Supreme Court essentially ruled that the Internet is fair game. Both you and your kids will have no problem finding pictures and videos of a bunch of naked people practicing their reproductive capabilities. What can parents and librarians do to filter this sex and junk (or, depending upon your perspective, extremely entertaining material) from minors? Net screening software seems to be a workable solution. Programs like Cyber Patrol and Surf Watch allow access only to sites deemed permissible by the software.

But this is just one small part of all the great information out there. Don't believe the hype about Internet sex scandals. Newspapers sell a lot more copies when the headlines read, "Child porn ring on the Internet broken."

Chat Chat Chat

Web **chat** is just coming into its own. It's called chat but people aren't talking, they are typing. The chat occurs in **chat rooms** where several users can simultaneously exchange written messages which appear on all the chat room participants' screens at the same time. When the messages appear as soon as you hit the SUBMIT button, this is called **real-time** chat because there is no delay. The whole element of simultaneous participation with users throughout the world makes web chat particularly engaging.

70% of AOL's over 8 million users partake in these online chat conversations between groups of AOL users all over America. Several web sites are adding these real-time, multi-user chat rooms. The chat room adds a tremendous community aspect to the Web. It's not about technology; it's about connecting to other people and sharing ideas, opinions, and bad jokes.

Women on the Web

In 1996 it was estimated that there were around 13.8 million women online, which was only 36.6% of the web population. By the end of 1997, the number is expected to increase to almost 24 million, or 40.2% of the total users, and by the year 2000, the number should grow to about 43 million women. This would bring the ratio to almost 47%. Thank goodness the Web is becoming less and less of a "guy only" thing. And from an economic perspective, women make over 70% of household purchases and are the most powerful consumers in the world.

Who is paying for all these web sites?

Several sites are trying to fund their existence through advertisements. In 1996, Web advertising became a $260 million dollar industry. Not bad considering that in 1991 there was less than 1 dollar spent on web advertising (remember the Web did exist until 1992!). But this pales in comparison to the $40 and $34 billion dollars which newspapers and television respectively generate in advertisement revenue annually. The number will go up in the years to come.

However, the majority of web sites are created and personally funded by individuals. These sites are home-made, simple, and inexpensive to produce. You'll know them when you see them.

Making your own web site

In the last couple of years, a whole new group of products have hit the market which show promise of making it easy for a person to put together a web page. Like everything else, to simply do it is really not that hard. To do it right is another story.

Making a web site can be really fun. Find a friend who has done it and can show you how. Your Internet Service Provider or Commercial Online Service will have a way for you to put your site up for the whole world to see. However, the majority of Internet users do not make web sites, they simply browse the Web. This is just fine.

Sphere 2: Dissemination of Traditional Big Media Information

There is no shortage of news on the Internet. Sports, headlines, weather, financial updates, stocks... From the New York Times to the San Jose Mercury News, information has found a comfortable new home. Most of it is free, besides the few papers and magazines such as Playboy and the Wall Street Journal which charge a fee. The online subscriptions fees vary in price but you can be assured the cost will be less than the printed version. The free ones, like CNN and ESPN, are funded through advertisements (what isn't funded through advertisements?).

A big reason for the popularity of the Web is that it drastically reduces transmission costs in comparison to radio broadcast, TV broadcast, and printing and distributing newspapers and magazines. Therefore, it is relatively inexpensive to go online and simply reformat the existing content to a web format.

If you're interested in another country, you can read their newspapers online. How about that? I lived a year in São Paulo, Brazil, as a Rotary International Exchange Student. I can keep up with what's going on in São Paulo by reading the *Folha de São Paulo* which is just one of several Brazilian newspapers and magazines online. Each country has a handful of its own. The Web takes people, places, and countries beyond traditional borders.

Hot new information vehicle

The Web is an incredible vehicle for sharing important news about the world in which we live. You can even tune-in to radio stations all over the world from the Web. The other day I was listening to my favorite channel in São Paulo, Brazil. (*You need to get a special* **plug-in** *for this as well as have computer speakers. Go to the Real Audio/Video home page, http://www.real.com to find out more*). Traditional media lines are rapidly disappearing between TV, newspapers, and radio as they rush to unite in one place. This is not a passing fad. TV had its critics in the beginning who also grossly underestimated its potential.

The Mars Pathfinder Site (http://mpfwww.jpl.nasa.gov)

The most popular web site so far has been NASA's Jet Propulsion Laboratory Mars Pathfinder site. On July 8, 1997, the site received an astonishing number of visitors (millions and millions). In this day and age of Web commercialism, it's good to see such an international interest in the pursuit of science. And in general, this example highlights the power of getting the information you want, when you want it. Most news stories disappear after a few days or weeks. The Mars pathfinder site is still there and you can access it any time you want, day or night. As NASA updates the information, you can research your favorite areas of interest and be your own filter of news and information.

Research

When it comes to research, the Web is the world's biggest library. The average person expands his or her ability to obtain information by leaps and bounds. This is the real power of the Internet and especially the Web. No place is too far away, no interest too small, no topic too esoteric. There is plenty of space for everyone's ideas, recipes, research papers, news articles, headlines, discoveries, and just good-old-fashioned opinions about those ideas, recipes, research papers, news articles, etc.

Don't Push Me

Another Web advancement blossoming in 1997 was this new way of having information "pushed" to you rather than your having to go out and get it for yourself. Typically when you use the Web, you have to make decisions all the time. This **push technology** is trying to make the Web a lot like television. You sit back and relax and it automatically comes to your computer. Pointcast (www.pointcast.com) is perhaps the most well known of the push technology companies. They have a special program which automatically sends you news updates, which you customize to your preferences ahead of time. How do they make their money? Hint: it begins with an A.

Sphere 3: A Powerful Distribution/Commerce Tool

Let's face it, we're Americans and we love to buy things. Capitalism boils in our blood and shopping is a celebration of our culture. We can go to the actual stores, or mail order, watch a television show about a product, or hear an advertisement over the radio. All of the major communication tools, TV, radio, and newspapers, are funded through advertisers who have something wonderful to sell you and me.

The Web is bursting right now with the ability to show you products and sell them to you right on the spot. From books to computer equipment to stocks to plane tickets, the Web holds the promise of true commerce. The Web is set up to do commerce. You can securely give your shipping information and credit card number to the online store by filling out a form in your browser. You submit this information with a simple click when you hit the SUBMIT button. In addition, most sites provide a toll free number for those hesitant to fill out the online forms. Your ordered products will come to you via the mail just as with mail ordering. You can specify FedEx, standard, or ground shipping.

Why use the Internet? Cheaper, quicker, and easier. And contrary to what you may have heard, 99% of it is safe. It's just like calling a catalog company, only rather than calling them with your information, you are sending it to them through your computer. (In Chapter 6 I mentioned that e-mail was unsafe. This is because anyone can read this information while it is in transit.) There are lots of companies and organizations working to make the Internet as safe as possible for commerce. This means that your credit card and billing information is transported in a special protected code (**encryption**) and is stored safely when it arrives at its destination.

On the other hand, beware of web scams and only shop at online stores with reputable names. How will you know? The most popular online stores become known and respected for their service and commitment to their customers. If a deal looks too good to be true, it probably is. The majority of Internet users are still hesitant to purchase goods online. This is understandable. In the future, when the average consumer has faith in the system, it will become more accepted and more common.

Online Malls and Stores

Vendors are opening up online stores because it's easy and relatively inexpensive. Soon enough you'll be able to find everything on the Web, from the obvious like music CDs, computer equipment, and software to the normal goods like toothpaste and toilet paper and groceries. Does this mean that everyone is going to be buying products online? No. Not even close. Some will, some won't.

No doubt you've heard of Amazon.com. If not, Amazon.com is the biggest book store on earth (at least that's what they say). If you know the book you want, there's a good chance they'll have it, can ship it to you in a couple of days, and will sell it to you for a better price. But this will certainly never replace the wonderful feeling of roaming around a cozy bookstore. The Web is not going to replace; it is merely going to supplement. Now you have more options. And just as mail order revolutionized several aspects of selling goods, so will the Web.

By cutting out the middleman, the Web does promise to offer good deals. It's certainly nicer to have this option than to not have it. I have only purchased one item online in the more than two years that I have been online: a book. I'm not worried about giving my credit card. I guess even for those people who work with the Internet for a living it takes time to adjust.

On the flip side, it's not an instant gold mine. IBM's World Avenue Mall flat out failed. This was just one of several companies who thought, "Oh, I'll just put it on the Web and get lots of customers." There's no one trick to success but value-added features and good content certainly can't hurt.

The Online Auction

A totally unique and profitable way of selling products was started by OnSale, Inc. (http://www.onsale.com). It is called the online auction. People submit their bids from all over the world and compete to get great prices on everything from computer parts to sports equipment. This goes to show how new technologies bring unique opportunities to the visionary who can translate one working model to a new paradigm. *The founder of OnSale, Inc. is none other than Jerry Kaplan, who wrote a neat book called* Startup *detailing his personal experiences during the rise and fall of his Silicon Valley startup company GO Computer. OnSale has enjoyed much greater success on the other hand.*

Online Brokers

If you already know the stock you want to buy, E*Trade (www.etrade.com) has commissions around $10.00. Not bad considering the alternatives. This has gained E*Trade more than 145,000 accounts. In the future, just about all the stock brokers, especially discount brokers, will be battling it out for your business. You'll see countless discount brokers and full brokerages houses turning to the Web. By offering a discount to its regular prices when you use the Web, Charles Schwab has already opened 800,000 online accounts. Not bad...

Where the real money is—the Intranet.

While I'm talking about all these web sites which you can access, I thought I'd bring up the ones you can't access. These are the web sites which companies publish for their own internal organizations. They are called Intranets, which is an adaptation of *inter* (meaning between) to *intra* (meaning inside). You may have wondered how software companies make money when all they do is give away free software on the Internet. They make their money selling these products to companies and large organizations. They give the product away to you on the Internet to gain name recognition as well as to demonstrate the usefulness of their product. Netscape is eying the **enterprise network** (central network of a company) as their new home.

There are big bucks in the Intranet. Companies have countless information problems which the Web paradigm is solving. I personally have designed a few of these systems and can clearly see their advantages. Think about how much information each company needs to distribute throughout its organization: employee manuals, technical details, operating instructions, time and project tracking, and on and on. The Web technologies applied to the Intranet makes it faster, easier, and cheaper. Under the new paradigm, when you make a small change you don't have to reprint 20,000 new copies of your employee manual.

Telecommuting

I work at home several days a week by using the Internet to access the computers at work and our company Intranet. I am able to accomplish just about everything from home besides face-to-face meetings. This is called **telecommuting** (you use your telephone line rather than a car to commute) and you can bet your favorite hat that this will become much more popular and standard in the years to come. It reduces the amount of cars, pollution, and commuting time wasted, plus you can work in your pajamas, so this improves worker efficiency too. For some jobs this simply won't work, but for many it can, does, and will.

The Firewall

I can't talk about the Intranet and telecommuting without mentioning the **firewall** too. A firewall is a barrier between the Internet and the Intranet. When a company connects its internal network to the Internet, it is exposing all of its computers to the nasty world of computer thieves and hackers who would just love to steal confidential information and wreak havoc. Just as a firewall in your car protects you from your engine, the software firewall protects organizations from the evil forces on the other side of the network. Firewall sales have increased dramatically within the last few years.

Here's an example of the firewall's usefulness. If the CIA had a better firewall it would have prevented hackers from breaking into their network and changing their home page to read "The Central Stupid Agency." This incident occurred in the beginning of 1997. The FBI fell victim to a similar attack. Kind of makes you wonder...

Online Privacy Rights

In concluding this section about the heart and soul of the Web, I want to mention one more important issue facing us all, our rights. Because the Web is so new, there are several potential opportunities for government infringement upon our rights. For instance, the FBI came up with a "clipper chip" which allows them to gain greater access to wiretaps for eavesdropping. The FBI also planned on adding massive wiretap capabilities to the telephone system. Basically, they would like as much access as possible to information. There is a fine line between serving the security interests of the country and eavesdropping. The Communications Decency Act threatened our First Amendment rights which was why a Federal Court ruled it unconstitutional.

Thankfully there are organizations dedicated to protecting your rights to privacy. Two of the most well known are the Electronic Privacy Information Center (http://www.epic.org) and the Electronic Frontier Foundation (http://www.eff.org). They are committed to serving the citizens of the United States and the world. As the Internet and Web push new frontiers, it's reassuring to have folks fighting hard to protect all of our inalienable rights. Our forefathers would be proud and certainly amazed at all this technology.

Almost done!

Can you believe it? We have just completed a bird's eye view of the Internet and the Web. If I did a good job, you are neither frustrated nor confused about the technology nor mad at me for wasting your time. I just have a few words left about the future of the Internet.

11

On the Horizon

The never ending flight of future days.
JOHN MILTON
1608–1674

Why would we want to talk about the future? Everything we covered is going on right now, so we don't have to wait to use it. And besides, it's a gorgeous Sunday afternoon in San Francisco and I'm going to ride my bike down to Ocean Beach and jump in the warm El Niño ocean. So I'll be brief.

On the horizon await a couple of advancements which could improve our capabilities with the Internet. **Cable modems** which hook into your TV cable lines rather than your phone lines are up to twenty times faster than today's fastest modem. This would open up a whole new world and increase the speed of what we see by several factors. It would add an amazing new dimension to multimedia and the Internet. But don't hold your breath. This could take many more years.

Several companies, including AT&T, are working to improve the **Voice-over-IP** which translates into using the Internet for phone calls. What's so great about this? You do not need to pay one penny for the phone calls. The first time I heard about this was in 1994. A friend at work would talk to his wife in Sweden a couple nights a week for three hours at a time. They used the Internet telephone which he told me sounded like a shortwave radio. But it was free. They've made vast improvements in the last couple of years. The real area of interest for this technology is not for the home consumer but for businesses. Right now it is common for a business to maintain two separate systems, their computer system and their phone system. One system is easier and less expensive than two.

Then there's the 3D technology for the Web called **VRML** which stands for **V**irtual **R**eality **M**arkup **L**anguage. VRML has the ability to create 3D multi-user environments. The biggest player in this arena is Silicon Graphics, the company which brought all those cool special effects to movies like *Terminator II* and *The Abyss*. Is this happening now? Yes. Can you see it now? Yes. Do I know anyone who uses it? No. You'll read about VRML or maybe see it on the news. VRML is the next step when dealing with the organization of information. We're visual creatures and these 3D worlds show us what we now have to put together for ourselves. I have a feeling something good will come of this. The real question is when.

If you have a television you can buy a a little box which connects your TV to the Internet. It's not nearly the same quality as a half-way decent computer screen, but it only costs a couple hundred dollars. **WebTV** is just starting to find its way into the American home. This may catch on; then again it may not. And for those who don't have a lot of money we have the **Network Computer** (**NC**) from Oracle (our friends who make the database). This inexpensive computer, around $300–$500, will automatically set itself up, get the programs it needs, and fix itself too. You won't have to know a thing, unlike with today's computers.

And finally we have the **webified household appliances**. You may have seen the Xerox TV commercial in which this guy dressed in a funky suit explains how you can use your Web browser to interact with your Xerox copier and fax machine at work to staple, send a fax, collate, etc. Along the same lines, in the future, lots of household appliances will come with the capability to interact in such a way—blenders, VCRs, your oven, door locks, and several common systems in your home. What does this mean for you? Now, your thief will be able to have a warm cup of coffee waiting for him inside your home after he opens your front door with the code he stole from the Internet.

And last, but certainly not least, there is **Java**, the new Internet-based computer programming language from Sun Microsystems. What's so hot about Java? First of all, the name. It's catchy (computer programmers have the stereotype of drinking lots of coffee) unlike other computer programming languages such as

BASIC, C and *C++*. Saying a program was written in Java means about as much to you as saying your car engine is constructed of a special light-weight alloy. What do you care as long as it runs fine? But for techy folks, Java is a great tool to make all kinds of computer programs. The best part of Java is that software programmers can create a single program and it will run on every kind of operating system in the exact same way. This will eliminate the differences between Mac, Windows, and several other operating systems too. You'll be hearing lots about Java in the future.

But enough with the future. Let's get on with today's Internet. So, Mom and Dad, and other newcomers to the Internet arena, this completes our tour. Now it's time for you to find your own path. Remember, you are not alone. There are people who want to help you out every step of the way from your friends to the companies who are selling you their products and services.

You'll do just fine. Happy trails!

A Friendly Glossary

Here are the core Internet words and terms and their respective definitions. I have included a few additional terms which I did not mention in this guide. I thought they would be helpful for your reference. I wish this list could have been a lot shorter but all the techy folks in the Internet field need something to do so they create acronyms and new terms. Please do not take them too seriously!

address book A collection of names and e-mail addresses which you can set up in your e-mail program. This makes it easy to send friends, family, and/or acquaintances the same message with just one click.

analog Describes data with quantities which continuously vary. An analog clock has hands whereas a **digital** clock has exact values.

anonymous ftp A way to **download** files on the Internet from another system without having to have a personal account on that system (anonymously). Please see **ftp**.

applet A basic building block of Java, the new programming language for the Internet. Applets are little programs which run in your web **browser** and do all kinds of dynamic things.

archie An Internet service which helps you find the names of **anonymous ftp** sites which have a file for which you are searching. The main search engines take care of this and you can use a **browser** to access this service.

Arpanet The original network started by the United States Department of Defense Advanced Research Project Agency back in 1968 which grew into the Internet.

article A **Usenet** message that gets posted to a **newsgroup**. You will read and post articles when you use Usenet.

ASCII A standard binary code for letters, numbers and special symbols developed by the American Standards Committee which can be recognized by all computer programs.

attach To "paper clip" a file in an e-mail program so that the file gets sent with your e-mail message.

attachment The "paper clipped" file which you will send or receive with an e-mail message. Make sure the receiver of your attachment has the right program to be able to read the attachment.

author In **Usenet**, a person who composes a message and posts it to a newsgroup.

backbone The really big pipes of the Internet which are owned by the large telecommunications companies such as AT& T, MCI, Sprint, and the large **Internet Service Providers**. They are the highest-speed pipes connecting the Internet computers together.

bandwidth The measure of how much info computers on the Internet can transmit and receive. Small bandwidth = a little. High bandwidth = lots.

baud A term for describing the speed of modems. Nowadays people use **bps**, or bits per second. Baud is just another confusing term which you do not need to know.

binary file A file that contains data that is not plain text and needs a special program to interpret what it is.

binary system A mathematical number system based on the digits 0 and 1. It's obligatory for every book about computers to have this.

bit Stands for "binary digit." A bit can either be on or off, and is represented by a 0 or 1. Does this concern you? No.

body The main part of an **e-mail** message, an **Usenet article**, a **web page**, and most animals.

bookmark list The list you make to save your favorite web locations. You can add to as well as delete locations from your list and store them in all kinds of orders and folders. This makes your life easier.

Boolean search Using "and" and "or" words in your search for a subject or a word.

bps **Bits** per second. The measure of your modem's speed. The bigger the number, such as 33.6 K, the faster the modem transmits.

browser The program used for going around the Internet to see **web pages**. Browser comes from "browsing around."

byte A group of 8 **bits**, or binary digits as the geeks refer to them. It's essential to have this in all computer books.

cable modems Modems which use cable lines to connect to the Internet. These are really fast in comparison with today's telephone **modems**.

cache The storage area which your **browser** uses to hold recently accessed files. This makes **web pages** come up much quicker. You can adjust the size of this storage area.

case insensitive Not distinguishing between uppercase and lowercase letters. E-mail addresses are case insensitive.

case sensitive The opposite of **case insensitive** or distinguishing between lowercase and uppercase letters. **Web addresses** are case sensitive.

CGI Common Gateway Interface. Don't ask, and I won't tell.

chat room A way to communicate with several other people at the same time using the Internet.

client A program which accesses resources from a **server**. Just as in a restaurant, the client asks and the server gets.

Commercial Online Service Member-only services which provide special forums in addition to access to the Internet. They usually change a flat monthly fee. *Compuserve*, *Prodigy*, and *America Online* are some well known ones.

configure To set up your computer system and programs.

cross-posting Within **Usenet**, to post an **article** to more than one **newsgroup**.

cyberspace A funky term referring to all the info and communication out there in the Internet.

cybersquatting Reserving a **domain** name with the intention of selling it.

database A program which stores information and optimizes it for quick retrieval.

digital Data which is represented by discrete numbers. So a digital watch is always exact whereas an **analog** watch with moving hands is not.

directory A fancy word for a computer "folder" which stores computers files and other computer "folders."

DNS Please see **Domain Name System**.

DNS server A server that translates **domain** names into **IP addresses**.

domain The main part of an Internet address which gets translated into a computer telephone number by the DNS server. sunshinedaydream.com is my domain for Sunshine Daydream.

Domain Name System Popularly referred to as **DNS**. An Internet service that translates an address from a **domain** name to an **IP address** (computer telephone number) and vice versa. sunshinedaydream.com gets translated into 206.40.77.07 by the DNS.

download Transferring files from another computer to your computer.

e-mail Electronic mail.

encrypt To write in a special protected code to insure privacy.

extension A short suffix tagged on to the end of a file name which helps identify what it is. For text files on the internet you will commonly see .htm, .html, .txt and for graphics .jpg, .jpeg, .gif.

enterprise network The main computer network of a company.

FAQ Frequently Asked Questions. A compilation of the most common questions and answers to those questions. You'll see this all over the Internet, from **Usenet newsgroups** to **web sites**.

file A computer file is a basic document which the computer reads and writes.

file transfer protocol Please see **FTP**.

flame A flame is an abusive response to a posting on **Usenet**.

form A form on the Web is similar to a form in paper—it allows you to enter information which you send to the web site whose form you are filling out.

FTP File Transfer Protocol. A set of rules, or **protocol**, for transfering files between computers.

frequently asked question list Please see FAQ.

geographical domain A two-letter **top-level domain** based on an abbreviation for a particular country. In gilbertogil.com.br the br is the geographical domain and it stands for Brazil.

getting online Using a computer to "talk" to other computers on the Internet.

gopher An Internet service which I did not mention in this book because you probably don't need to know about it.

graphical user interface This is nothing more than what you see when you use a computer program in 1998. All the colorful buttons and so on. You visually interact with the interface. Referred to as **GUI**.

group A discussion group in **Usenet**. Commonly referred to as **newsgroup**.

GUI Acronym for **graphical user interface**.

hard drive The place for storing your computer programs and files.

hardware Physical computer parts such as the computer, the monitor, the keyboard, modem and so on.

header All the extra information at the top of a mail message and **Usenet article**. You don't need to pay attention to it (it's just technical stuff).

helper application A program that extends ("helps" out) the functionality of a **browser**. This shortcoming will be going away as browsers mature.

home page A home page has two different meanings. It is both the main page of a web site as well as the location your **browser** goes each and every time it is started.

host A computer connected to the Internet.

hotlinks The words and pictures you can click on which take you to other sources of information on the **Web**.

HTML Hyper Text Markup Language. A special format for a text file which the **browser** reads and is instructed how to format the **web page**.

http This stands for hyper text transfer protocol. It's what identifies a **web page** or web resource.

hyper text markup language Please see HTML.

hypertext Information on the Web which specifies links to other web pages, sites, and other web resources like graphics and sounds.

HyperText Transfer Protocol This is the **protocol** (set of rules) used to transfer web pages which are composed of **hypertext**. See **http**.

icon A little computer graphic that you click on to open a program or computer file.

Internet When we say the Internet, we are talking about a worldwide system of computers, the information on those computers, and the people all over the world accessing and sharing that information. The Internet = **the Net**.

Internet Protocol See IP.

Internet Service Provider An Internet Service Provider, or ISP for short, provides access to the Internet for a monthly fee.

InterNIC The Internet Network Information Center. The most complete **Domain Name Server** on the Internet.

Intranet Web sites which companies publish for their own internal organization's use amongst employees.

IP A part of the TCP/IP protocols which moves the packets of info composing all those cool text, graphic and multimedia files from one computer to another on the Internet. IP is an acronym for **Internet Protocol**.

IP address This is nothing more than an Internet computer number. Think of this as a telephone number for an Internet computer. The IP address for Sunshine Daydream is 206.40.77.07.

ISDN Another way to get connected to the Internet. It's more expensive than the standard way of getting connected and it's much more of a hassle too. ISDN stands for Integrated Services Digital Network.

ISP See Internet Service Provider.

Java The new Internet-based, computer programming language from Sun Microsystems.

kbps Kilo (thousands of) **bits** per second. 28.8 kbps = 28,800 **bps**.

LAN Local Area Network. It rhymes with **WAN**.

link A connection from one web resource to another. Also called a **hotlink**.

Local Area Network A happy group of computers connected to each other by cable and able to communicate with one another.

local host Your computer is the local host when you are connected to the Internet. Your local host accesses all the info on the **remote hosts** which are every other computer on the Internet but yours.

log in To start a new session with an Internet computer. When you get connected to the Internet, you will log in first.

log out To terminate your session with an Internet computer. When you're done using the Internet, you will log out. This takes place automatically.

login name This is the name you choose for your account with your **Internet Service Provider** or **Commercial Online Service**. This becomes your e-mail address.

lowercase The small letters abcdefghijklmnopqrstuvwxyz.

Mac A Macintosh computer. These are made by Apple computer.

mail client This is simply your local **e-mail** program.

mail server This is the program running on an Internet computer which gives your local **e-mail** program your mail. There are lots of mail servers strewn throughout the Internet constantly sending, receiving, and forwarding messages.

mailbox This is where you will receive your incoming **e-mail** just like the physical mailbox is for physical mail.

megabyte Millions of **bytes**.

megahertz Millions of whatever per second.

meg Abbreviation for **megabyte**.

Mime Multiple Internet Mail Extensions. I intentionally omitted this to confuse you less.

modem A device that allows you to connect your computer to a telephone line. It's an actual little box that plugs into your computer on one end and your telephone line on the other.

moderated A **Usenet newsgroup** whose postings are controlled by a person called a **moderator**. This keeps the quality high.

moderator The person who controls the messages (**articles**) which are posted to their **moderated newsgroup**.

mouse Of course you know what a computer mouse is!

multimedia Lots of media, like sound, video, pictures, music, and the works. A **multimedia system** can do all the fun stuff.

multimedia system A complete computer system including the computer, monitor, keyboard, mouse, and speakers which has the ability play audio and display computer graphics and video.

Net, the How some folks refer to the Internet.

network Two or more computers connected together and able to talk to one another.

Network Computer Inexpensive computers which hold the promise of simplifying the process of setting up and using a computer for the Internet.

news client This is the technical term for the **newsreader** program which you will use to read and post **Usenet** messages (**articles**).

news server The server program for **Usenet**. There are lots of these servers all talking to one another throughout the world. The news server talks to your **newsreader** program.

newsgroup A discussion group within Usenet. There are over 16,000 of these individual discussion groups and more are added all the time.

newsreader The **client** program used to read **Usenet** messages (**articles**).

online Connected to the Internet.

operating system The computer program which operates the computer. There are several kinds of operating systems such as Apple Computer's System 7 and 8 and Microsoft Windows.

organizational domains The three-letter **top-level domain**s (.com, .edu, .gov, .int, .mil, .net, and .org) seen in Internet addresses.

packets The small packages of data which the computers of the Internet send to one another using **TCP/IP protocols**.

password This is the secret code you choose to protect the account you open with an **Internet Service Provider** or **Commercial Online Service**. Make sure your password is easy enough for you to remember and hard enough for someone else not to be able to guess.

PC Personal computer. IBM made the original PCs but now you can buy clones from several other companies.

plug-in Special software parts which extend the functionality of your browser.

point of presence The location you will dial into to connect with your **Internet Service Provider** or **Commercial Online Service**. Some services offer multiple points of presence in other cities, states and even countries.

point-to-point protocol See PPP.

POP 1. an abbreviation for **point of presence**. 2. **Post Office Protocol**. The language your local e-mail program speaks to your **mail server**.

Post Office Protocol See POP.

posting A message that's posted to a **newsgroup** in **Usenet**. Commonly referred to as an **article**.

PPP Point-to-Point Protocol. How your computer and the computer on the other end of the phone line speak (**the protocol**) to one another.

processor The engine of your computer. The more powerful the processor, the faster your computer operates.

protocol A code (set of rules) which must be agreed upon by those who use it.

push technology An Internet technology which automatically sends ("pushes") information to your computer at selected intervals.

RAM This is the special memory for running your computer programs. The more RAM you have, the more programs you can run at the same time. It stands for Random Access Memory.

real-time A fancy way of saying "without delay."

remote host All the other computers on the Internet besides yours which is the **local host**.

router A specialized computer which connects one network to another.

search engine A search engine is an Internet directory or card catalog of information existing on the Internet. They are the **web sites** you'll go to on **the Web** to find everything you need. These include *Yahoo!, Excite, InfoSeek,* and *Lycos* to name a few.

server Servers respond to requests from **client programs**. There are all kinds of servers, such as **mail servers, web servers,** and **news servers**.

signature A special area of personalized text which can automatically be included in each **e-mail** message and **Usenet posting**.

Simple Mail Transfer Protocol See **SMTP**.

SMTP Simple Mail Transfer Protocol. The language that mail servers all throughout the Internet speak to one another.

snail mail A wry term for regular mail mocking the speed of delivery in comparison to **e-mail**.

software Computer code telling the computer what to do and how to behave.

spam Junk **e-mail** messages.

subdomain One part of the **domain** name. In http://www.gilbertogil.com.br, gilberto, com, and br are all subdomains of the domain gilbertogil.com.br.

subjects In **Usenet**, the titles of the messages (**articles**).

subscribe When using **Usenet**, you subscribe to a particular newsgroup or groups to select them and read the messages (**articles**) contained within.

surf As in "surf the Web." To **browse** around the Web.

TCP Transmission Control Protocol. One of the **TCP/IP protocols** which coordinates flow of **packets** from one Internet computer to another Internet computer.

TCP/IP The common language which all the computers on the Internet speak to one another. It really stands for **Transmission Control Protocol** and **Internet Protocol**.

Telecommuting Working at home using the Internet to access your company's resources and **Intranet**.

text file A file which every computer can read because it is so simple. **Binary files** on the other hand, require special computer programs for interpretation.

top-level domain The most general **subdomain** in an Internet address. The most common top-level domains are .com, .org, and .edu. In gold@sunshine-daydream.com, the .com is the top-level domain. .com stands for company.

unmoderated In **Usenet**, a **newsgroup** which has no one (a **moderator**) filtering the content of the group.

unsubscribe In **Usenet**, unsubscribing is your way of indicating that you no longer want to read messages (**articles**) within a **newsgroup**.

upload Transferring files from your computer to another computer.

uppercase The capital letters ABCDEFGHIJKLMNOPQRSTUVWXYZ.

URL The techy way of saying **web address**. URL stands for Uniform Resource Locator.

Usenet Usenet stands for User's Network. Usenet is a worldwide system of discussion groups covering a myriad of topics.

uuencode A system which encodes **binary** data as **ASCII** text. Folks use these programs to put pictures in text-only messages (**articles**) in **Usenet**.

Voice-over-IP The technology that uses the Internet for regular telephone calls.

VRML Virtual Reality Markup Language. A Web technology that allows users to simultaneously participate in 3-D, multi-user worlds.

WAN Please see **Wide Area Network**.

Web, the An Internet service which relies on **browsers** accessing resources in the form of text, pictures, video, and audio from **web servers**. The Web is short for the **World Wide Web**.

web address The address for a web site such as www.sunshinedaydream.com. The real name for this is **URL** or Uniform Resource Locator.

web page All the individual pages of information which comprise **the Web**. You view web pages with a browser. A web page can contain text, sound, animation, video and more.

web site A group of **web pages** usually organized by a particular topic or subject. Sunshine Daydream is a web site for outdoor adventure sports.

WebTV A special box which adapts your TV for Internet usage.

Wide Area Network A network comprised of more than one local area networks or **LAN**s. Commonly referred to as **WAN**.

word processor A computer program for composing letters, books, and papers.

World Wide Web The Web.

WWW Abbreviation for **World Wide Web**. So, in http://www.sunshinedaydream.com, now you know what the www means.

Come visit our website for

Walk with me through the Internet

http://www.walkwithme.com

Connect with others just like yourself!

Helpful Hints

Helpful Links

Colorful Illustrations

Online Postcards

Order Information

and more...